Edward Bulwer-Lytton

Twayne's English Authors Series

Herbert Sussman, Editor

Northeastern University

TEAS 420

EDWARD BULWER-LYTTON
(1803–1873)
*Portrait by G. F. Watts. Reprinted courtesy of
the National Portrait Gallery, London*

Edward Bulwer-Lytton

By James L. Campbell, Sr.

*University of California
at Santa Barbara*

Twayne Publishers • Boston

*To Lady Campbell
and William E. Harrold*

Edward Bulwer-Lytton

James L. Campbell, Sr.

Copyright © 1986 by G.K. Hall & Co.
All Rights Reserved
Published by Twayne Publishers
A Division of G.K. Hall & Co.
70 Lincoln Street
Boston, Massachusetts 02111

Copyediting supervised by Lewis DeSimone
Book production by Lyda E. Kuth
Book design by Barbara Anderson

Typeset in 11 pt. Garamond
by Modern Graphics, Inc., Weymouth, Massachusetts

Printed on permanent/durable acid-free paper
and bound in the United States of America

Library of Congress Cataloging in Publication Data

Campbell, James L.
   Edward Bulwer-Lytton.

   Twayne's English authors series; TEAS 420)
   Bibliography: p. 144
   Includes index.
   1. Lytton, Edward Bulwer Lytton, Baron, 1803–1873—Criticism and
interpretation. I. Title. II. Series.
PR4938.C3   1986   823′.8   85–24887
ISBN 0–8057–6914–5

Contents

About the Author

James L. Campbell teaches at the University of California at Santa Barbara and is a specialist in Victorian fiction, especially minor nineteenth-century British novels. He has published articles on Sir Arthur Conan Doyle, Mrs. Henry Wood, Mrs. J. H. Riddell, Joseph Sheridan Le Fanu, Sir Walter Scott, W. Olaf Stapledon, G. P. Serviss, and John Taine. At present he is engaged in writing a multivolume critical history of Victorian sensational fiction. During 1978 and 1979 Dr. Campbell was an International Knapp Fellow at the British Library in London, where he did research on rare Victorian novels.

Dr. Campbell received bachelor of arts degrees in modern European history (1971) and English literature (1972), as well as a master's and a Ph.D. in English (1974 and 1983), all from the University of Wisconsin—Milwaukee. He has taught at the University of Kansas and at Graceland College.

Preface

At the time of his death in 1873, Edward Bulwer-Lytton was recognized as one of England's greatest writers, a view, however, that the ensuing years failed to sustain. By the turn of the century his reputation, like those of many other Victorian writers, had greatly declined. Early twentieth-century critics condemned him for his false sentiment and poor character psychology. Some complained that his overly romantic style (called "Bulwerese") detracted from his books, that his aesthetic doctrine of the ideal and the real seemed incomprehensible, that his many prefaces to his books contained only self-advertisement, and that his exploration of so many fictional genres prevented him from excelling in any one form. Generally Bulwer seemed but a clever literary opportunist who sought wide popularity by giving the public what it wanted. Recent work on Bulwer by Robert Lee Wolff, Edwin Eigner, and Allan C. Christensen, however, opposes this view, arguing that he was a dedicated and serious writer who produced books of genuine literary distinction and lasting influence.

This book advances the view of Bulwer first expressed by Victorian novelist Anthony Trollope, who saw him as an intellectual writer and not merely as a popular storyteller. The following chapters seek to illuminate the artistry and intellectual power of his writings through a close reading of his novels and stories and a careful study of his essays, letters, and prefaces. Such scrutiny sheds light on his continuous preoccupation with the integrity and vitality of ideas.

In this study I examine the entire canon of Bulwer's fiction, provide a critical analysis of his books, chronicle the periodization of his artistic development, and evaluate him within the larger context of Victorian literature—his contribution, influence, merit, significance, and rank as a nineteenth-century man of letters. Chapter 1 describes Bulwer's life, early Byronic poetry, and plays. The succeeding chapters group his novels by genre, analyzing his Byronic apprenticeship to literature and his early novels (chapter 2), his crime and Newgate novels (chapter 3), his bildungsromane and metaphysical romances (chapter 4), his historical novels and costume romances (chapter 5), his domestic novels of real life (chapter 6),

EDWARD BULWER-LYTTON

his occult and scientific romances (chapter 7), and his place in
Victorian literature (chapter 8).

No account of Bulwer could be undertaken without the guidance
of earlier books about him by his son, Robert, first earl of Lytton;
his grandson, Victor, second earl of Lytton; T. H. S. Escott; Michael
Sadleir; Robert Lee Wolff; Edwin Eigner; and Allan C. Christensen,
all of which I have consulted. This study is based on a thesis sub-
mitted for the degree of doctor of philosophy at the University of
Wisconsin—Milwaukee in 1983. I am especially grateful to Professor
William E. Harrold, chairman of my dissertation committee, for
his guidance, and to my other readers, Professors James Kuist, Kay
Whitford, and Frank Campenni, for their criticism of the original
manuscript. Also, I greatly benefited from discussions on Bulwer
with Professor George Worth, Professor Max K. Sutton, and Dr.
Ann M. Ross of the University of Kansas, who provided me with
added insights on Bulwer and Victorian fiction. I owe a debt of
thanks to Professor Arthur L. Gardner, acting dean of faculty at
Graceland College, who found financial assistance for the preparation
of the typescript in an era of restricted budgets. And to Shirley
Dement goes my appreciation for typing the manuscript. Lastly, I
am indebted to Herbert Sussman, my field editor, whose suggestions
improved my book.

James L. Campbell, Sr.

University of California at Santa Barbara

Acknowledgments

The author and publisher are grateful to the following for permission to quote from their works: *Strange Stories and Other Explorations in Victorian Fiction* by Robert Lee Wolff, © 1971 by Gambit Press; *The Life of Edward Bulwer, First Lord Lytton* by Victor, second earl of Lytton, copyright 1913 by Macmillan and Co., Ltd.; *The Metaphysical Novel in England and America: Dickens, Bulwer, Hawthorne, Melville,* by Edwin M. Eigner, © 1978 by the University of California Press; *Edward Bulwer-Lytton: The Fiction of New Regions* by Allan Conrad Christensen, © 1976 by the University of Georgia Press; *The Newgate Novel, 1830–1847,* by Keith Hollingsworth, © 1963 by Wayne State University Press.

Chronology

1842   *Zanoni.*

1843   *The Last of the Barons.*

1846   *Lucretia.*

1847   *A Word to the Public* as a defense of his crime fiction.

1848   *Harold; King Arthur.* Daughter Emily dies.

1849   *The Caxtons.*

1851   Joins Conservative party.

1852–1866   Returns to Parliament as conservative member for Hertford.

1853   *My Novel.*

1858   *What Will He Do with It?*

1858–1859   Secretary of state for the colonies in Lord Derby's conservative administration.

1862   *A Strange Story.*

1863   *Caxtoniana.*

1866   Raised to the peerage as Baron Lytton. *The Lost Tales of Miletus.*

1869   *Walpole; The Odes and Epodes of Horace.* Receives the order of St. Michael and St. George.

1871   *The Coming Race.*

1873   *Kenelm Chillingly.* 18 January, dies at Torquay. *The Parisians.*

1876   *Pausanias the Spartan.*

Chapter One
Life and Times

Among Victorian novelists none more stoutly defended the literary romance than Edward Bulwer-Lytton, and few led more singularly romantic lives. Little about Bulwer can be considered prosaic. At one time or other he was a fashionable dandy, an advanced political radical, a grand patron in the Rosicrucian Brotherhood, a cabinet minister, a nominee to the throne of Greece, and a popular novelist and playwright. His experiences exemplified what sensational novelist Wilkie Collins called the romance of real life, the "extraordinary accidents and events which happen to few men."[1]

Such an event occurred to Bulwer in 1824, when he met a beautiful gypsy fortune-teller while on a walking tour of the English Lake District. After reading Bulwer's palm, she told him, "You will not have the honours you count on now. . . . You'll know scandal and slander . . . be spoken ill of where you least deserve. . . . Your best friends and your worst enemies will be women. You'll hunger for love all your life, and you will have much of it, but less satisfaction than sorrow. . . . You will be your own enemy!"[2] This prophecy, later fictionalized in his third novel, *The Disowned* (1828), proved remarkably accurate. While Bulwer achieved great literary success, he lived a lonely, unhappy life, secretly hungering for the love and sympathy of an ideal woman. Many who knew him recognized that Bulwer was often his own worst enemy, as his personal reserve, family pride, and oversensitivity to criticism subjected him to public scandal and literary slander.

Edward George Earle Lytton Bulwer (known after 1843 as Bulwer-Lytton and after 1866 as Baron Lytton of Knebworth) was born on 25 May 1803 at 31 Baker Street, London. His parents were Elizabeth Barbara Bulwer (née Lytton) (1773–1843), heiress of the Robinson and Lytton families of Knebworth in Hertfordshire, and General William Earle Bulwer (1757–1807) of Heydon Hall in Norfolk. His father, commander of the 106th Norfolk Rangers, descended from an ancient family residing in Norfolk since 1066, when the founder of the family, a Dane named Turold Bulver, received lands at Wooddalling from Aymer de Valence for his services to William the Conqueror. General Bulwer married Miss Lytton on 21 June 1798, but his violent temper, inflamed by chronic gout, led to a quarrel with his mother-in-law that terrified his wife. He eventually separated from his wife and took up residence at St. Lawrence near Ramsgate. Acting on family advice, Mrs. Bulwer applied to the Court of Chancery and obtained both the guardianship of her children and the costs for their maintenance. In 1804 the government appointed Bulwer military commander of Lancashire, where he undertook preparations to defend the area against French invasion. Because of his services to the nation, General Bulwer hoped to be raised to the peerage as the first Lord South Erpingham, but he died on 7 July 1807 before the government could reward his aspirations. His widow moved to London with her four-year-old son, sending to school the two older boys, William (1799–1877), who inherited Heydon Hall, and Henry, later Lord Dalling (1801–72), who distinguished himself in the Foreign Office. Because of poor health, Edward remained at home with his mother, who lavished on him all the love she could no longer give to her husband or to her other, absent children.

Education and Byronic Youth

Young Bulwer's education began at home, where his mother frequently recited poetry to him—especially Goldsmith and Gray—and read stories from Homer about the siege of Troy. The boy learned to read quite early and began to compose his own poetry at the age of seven, making him seem a prodigy to his family. In his unfinished *Autobiography,* Bulwer claimed that his first introduction to books arose from the death of his eccentric maternal grandfather, Richard Warburton Lytton, who died on 30 December 1810. A famous Latin scholar and friend of Dr. Samuel Parr, Lytton possessed a large library that after his death was removed to his daughter's house in Montagu Square to be sold to pay his debts. Browsing among his grandfather's books, Bulwer "looked and lingered—read and wondered," getting "ankle-deep in the great slough of Metaphysics."[3] In 1812 he asked his mother: "Pray, are you not sometimes overcome by the sense of your own identity?"[4] To which she replied that it was high time he go to school. Accordingly, he went to Dr. Ruddock's school at Fulham, but because of ill treatment he was transferred to Rottingdean to study under Dr. Hooker. Here he read Scott, fell in love with Byron's poetry, started a weekly magazine, became the best pugilist in the school, and showed such physical energy and intellectual vigor that in 1818 Hooker advised Mrs. Bulwer to send her son to a public school, where he might benefit from a wider sphere of activity. In the mid-1840s Bulwer fictionalized these schoolboy scenes in his unfinished autobiographical novel, *Lionel Hastings,* describing himself as openly rebellious of all authority and discipline. While Hooker praised Bulwer for possessing "a mind of very extraordinary Compass," he warned that his high spirits might "prove the ruin of his character."[5]

Hoping to evade further education, Bulwer returned home determined to play the fashionable dandy in the neighborhood, but in 1819 his mother sent him to Ealing to study under the Reverend Charles Wallington in preparation for Cambridge. His new preceptor proved a perfect antidote to Bulwer's high spirits, as he was part priest and part soldier—a Tory and High Churchman who admired Sir Robert Peel. At Ealing Bulwer made progress in the classics, discussed politics, learned oratory, and acquired a love of letters. For his part, Wallington appealed to his student's idealism and love of history; he thought Bulwer a genius and encouraged him to publish his youthful verses. In April 1820 Mrs. Bulwer prevailed upon the London firm of J. Hatchard and Son to print a collection of her son's poems under the title of *Ismael: An Oriental Tale, with Other Poems.* Later Bulwer depreciated these poems as mere versemaking; he noted that *Ismael* began "Byron-like, with 'Tis Eve,' etc., and was thronged with bulbuls and palm trees."[6] Its sales proved even smaller than the volume, but he received a polite acknowledgment from Sir Walter Scott and an enthusiastic letter from Dr. Parr.

While at Ealing, Bulwer had a platonic love affair that profoundly shaped his life and gave rise to his lifelong romantic idealism. During the summer of 1820, he fell in love with a girl identified only as Lucy D——, who resided near Ealing. Having no mother or sister, she enjoyed a liberty of conduct equal to Bulwer's. Both were too young to speak of marriage, but they believed nature intended them for each other. They met secretly along the banks of the Brent until Lucy suddenly disappeared. This romantic disappointment threw Bulwer into a state of Byronic melancholy, leaving him depressed and indifferent to life. He declared that love was dead to him forever and that the freshness of his youth had been buried in the grave.[7] Three years later the girl sent him a deathbed letter, explaining that her father had forced her into a marriage with a man she never loved. Bulwer later provided further details in a poem entitled "The Tale of a Dreamer," written in 1824 and published privately two years later in Paris in *Weeds and Wildflowers*. To Bulwer Lucy confessed that despite attempts to smother her love, she had remained devoted to him; her approaching death, she hinted, arose from a broken heart. In her letter she asked him to visit her grave, and Bulwer made a pilgrimage to Ullswater in 1824, where he sought to exorcise the ghost that haunted his heart. After his all-night vigil, he felt reborn, recovering a more healthful mind and dedicating his life to literature. Recalling the episode years later, Bulwer claimed that the love they felt seemed "unlike the love of grown-up people, so pure and yet so passionate that never again can I feel any emotion comparable to its . . . tenderness."[8] Late in life, he retold the incident in *Kenelm Chillingly* (1873), one of his last novels. As Bulwer admitted in his *Autobiography,* this "stage of experience and feeling . . . contributed largely to render me whatever I have since become."[9] The girl at Ealing became the model for many of Bulwer's fictional heroines—young, idealized, fairylike girls, innocent and pure yet made interesting by their freedom from conventional social behavior.

His two years at Ealing (1819–21) provided Bulwer with the rudiments of Latin and Greek, sparked his interest in history, and sustained his love of books and reading. But he was woefully deficient in mathematics and had to go to St. Lawrence to brush up his skills with an Oxford tutor named Thomson. Bulwer entered Trinity College at Cambridge during the Easter term of 1822, but the next term he transferred to Trinity Hall, where he could be excused from college lectures as a fellow-commoner. "I went to college," he wrote later, "with a great fund of general reading, and habits of constant application" but "did nothing."[10] He became friends with Alexander Cockburn, later chief justice, who urged him to join the Union Debating Society. At the time, the Union comprised the leading undergraduates in the university—Winthrop Mackworth Praed, Charles Villiers, F. D. Maurice, Charles Buller, Benjamin Hall Kennedy, and Thomas Babington Macaulay. Bulwer participated in several debates, arguing on one occasion for greater liberty of the press, which became a lifelong interest. He won the

Chancellor's medal in July 1825 for a poem in English entitled "Sculpture." *Fraser's Magazine* noticed it and attacked its author in sharply personal terms, starting a long campaign of vilification against Bulwer in that periodical. In 1826 Bulwer took his B.A. degree, in 1835 he received his M.A., and in 1864 Cambridge University honored him with an LL.D. degree for his contribution to literature. While still at Cambridge, he began his apprenticeship to literature by publishing another collection of poems, *Delmour; or, A Tale of a Sylphid, and Other Poems* (1823). He also finished a draft of his first novel, *Falkland* (1827), completed the opening chapter of *Pelham* (1828), and filled a number of commonplace books that ultimately became the source of his masterly historical study, *England and the English* (1833).

Before beginning his literary career in earnest, Bulwer spent two years traveling. During 1824 he made his pilgrimage to Ullswater, visited Robert Owen's model factory, lived among gypsies for a week, called at Edinburgh, and returned to England by sea from Scotland. But the highlight of these adventures proved to be his brief infatuation with Lady Caroline Lamb. A popular novelist and Byron's former mistress, Lady Caroline interested Bulwer chiefly because of her graphic depictions of Byron, whom she made a beautiful monster, half demon and half demigod. In 1824 she was in her late thirties but looked far younger because of her childlike hairstyle of close curls. Gifted with remarkable powers of conversation, she appeared wildly original to the young Bulwer, combining infantine drollery with astute worldliness. Bulwer occasionally visited her at Brocket Park, which stood near his family's home at Knebworth. They corresponded frequently, and later he observed that her letters contained "a good deal of sentiment and romance which looked like love" but "never came to that."[11] At twenty-two Bulwer proved incapable of discerning the difference between sentiment and love, and when he grew more fascinated, she abruptly turned her attentions to another. He fled home, feeling that she had trifled with his affections and betrayed him. Only later could he recognize that Lady Caroline intended him no offense but was entirely the slave of impulse and caprice. Her sudden transports of sentiment were subject to misinterpretation by one so naive and inexperienced. In his effort to model his life after Byron, Bulwer wrongly assumed that he might replace him in Lady Caroline's affections. Eventually he resolved his romantic frustrations by fictionalizing these flirtations in two early novels, *Rupert de Lindsay* (1825) and *Lionel Hastings,* in which he portrayed her foibles with some charity.

A year later Bulwer accompanied his friend Frederick Villiers—the original of Henry Pelham in *Pelham*—to Boulogne, where he acted second in a duel before journeying on to Paris. According to his *Autobiography,* he was admitted "into circles not often open to foreigners of his age."[12] He became intimate with a few aristocratic families in the Faubourg St. Germain, being kindly received by the Marquise de La Rochejacquelein and her two daughters. Most of his introductions came from the Abbé Kinsela, an Irish Jesuit and confessor of Madame de Polignac, who tried to arrange a marriage between Bulwer and a well-born Parisian girl. But Mrs. Bulwer's horror of popery induced him to break off the affair and to decline further visits to the girl's family. He withdrew to Versailles, where he found solace in frequent riding and feverish verse writing. The product of his latest love affair was a third volume of poetry published in 1826 as *Weeds and Wildflowers.* These verses, like his earlier ones, are heavily derivative of Byron in both subject and style. At the end of April 1826, Bulwer left Paris and returned to London. While visiting his mother in Upper Seymour Street, Bulwer agreed to accompany her to an evening party, where he met a remarkably beautiful Irish girl named Rosina Doyle Wheeler, niece of General Sir John Doyle and protégée of Lady Caroline Lamb.

Marriage and Early Authorship

The attraction between Miss Wheeler and Bulwer was immediate. Bulwer had returned to England despondent and susceptible to further romantic attachments; Miss Wheeler appeared the perfect antidote to his Byronic world-weariness. In manner she displayed an easy self-assurance, a marked unconventionality of thought, and a vivacity in conversation set off by her native Irish wit. Clever and accomplished, Rosina was thoroughly in love with life. But her grandson later observed that her character bore some glaring defects: there was "an absence of dignity . . . and a want of respect either for herself or others."[13] Often she indulged a malicious humor, straining after comic effects both wearisome and irritating. These qualities arose from a dreadful childhood. Her father, Francis Massey Wheeler, married unwisely, uniting himself at seventeen to a girl of fifteen; the marriage failed after the birth of six children. Securing a deed of separation, Mrs. Wheeler took twelve-year-old Rosina to Caen, where they became the center of a small group of socialists and free-thinkers. But Rosina found little affection or happiness with her mother, and at seventeen she went to Ireland, where she lived with Miss Mary Greene, an old family friend. In contrast to Rosina's iconoclasm, Miss Greene was orthodox and straitlaced in outlook; she took offense at the girl's caustic wit and contempt for social conventions. As a consequence, Rosina soon grew tired of Ireland and went to live with her granduncle, Sir Francis Doyle, in London. There she met many of the literary lions of the age—poet Thomas Campbell, essayist Walter Savage Landor, and novelists Letitia Landon and Lady Caroline Lamb. Among them she first heard of Bulwer, who was spoken of as a fashionable dandy and coming young man of literary promise.

Throughout the summer the pair met, and in August they declared their love to each other. But Mrs. Bulwer, who had introduced the couple and encouraged their subsequent meetings, objected to any thought of marriage. Her opposition rested on Rosina's character, upbringing, and friends; she sought to prevent her son from marrying a woman unlikely to bring him happiness. Certainly no match could have been more inappropriate. Arguments arose between mother and son, creating bitterness on both sides. Throughout, Bulwer felt honorbound to defend Rosina. By invoking her authority rather than treating him with sympathy, Mrs. Bulwer ultimately drove her son to rebel. At first Bulwer broke off his engagement in deference to his mother, promising never to marry without her permission. But when he learned that Rosina was ill— perhaps suffering on his account—his resolve wavered. He rushed to her side, renewed their engagement, and felt more obliged to marry Rosina than to keep his promise to his mother. In a private memorandum written in 1846, Bulwer observed that "I married my wife against all my interests and prospects—not from passion, but from a sense of honour. She had given herself to me nearly a year before, and from that moment I considered myself bound to her."[14] On 30 August 1827 the couple exchanged vows at St. James's Church in London—but without his mother in attendance.

Following the wedding, the young couple leased Woodcot House in Reading, near a town with the ominous name of Nettlebed. They spent two happy years there, during which their first child, Emily, was born. For Bulwer early married life proved difficult, especially after his mother withdrew his allowance as a sign of her disapproval of his marriage. He had no income of his own and Rosina's income did not exceed £80 a year. While his older brother offered financial help, Bulwer was too proud to accept it, replying that "as I bake so will I brew."[15] Obligated to earn his own living, he subjected himself to prodigious literary exertions that injured his health and destroyed his chance for domestic happiness.[16]

In January 1829 the Bulwers moved to London, where they bought a home at 36 Hertford Street for £2,570 and spent a further £820 for redecoration. Their second child, Edward Robert—who became a distinguished career diplomat and poet—was born there on 8 November 1831. Between 1827 and 1835 their living expenses averaged £3,000 a year, and Bulwer set to work as a writer to provide Rosina with all the luxuries she so loved. The fashionable world in which the young couple moved revolved around expensive dinner parties, balls, masquerades, river parties to Richmond, evenings at Almacks, weekends in the country, trips to Goodwood and Ascot, soirées, and posh West End private clubs like the Carleton—in short, the glamorous world of privilege and politics, title and talent, dandies and fops. In such a world Bulwer found a source for his early fiction. He busied himself writing for all kinds of literary markets, from serious political periodicals to sentimental keepsakes, annuals, and books of beauty. Between 1827 and 1837 Bulwer completed thirteen novels, two long poems, one political pamphlet, four plays, a social history of England, a three-volume history of Athens, and all the tales collected in *The Student.* He wrote anonymously for the *Edinburgh Review,* the *Westminster Review,* the *Monthly Chronicle,* the *Examiner,* and the *Literary Gazette,* and he edited the *New Monthly Magazine* between 1831 and 1832.[17] Samuel Carter Hall, his subeditor, described Bulwer's amazing industry: "I have known him [to] write an article for the *New Monthly* overnight which I well knew he had not touched before late in the evening, but which was ready in the morning when I called for it."[18]

Despite his early interest in poetry, Bulwer launched his writing career and made his name among his contemporaries as a novelist. His gloomy Byronic romance, *Falkland,* appeared in 1827, arousing little interest among the public. But *Pelham,* its witty anti-Byronic successor about fashionable life, came out in June 1828 and after a slow start became the most popular novel of the season. Bulwer boasted that *Pelham* had put down the Byronic mania by substituting a more manly kind of foppery. It introduced the fashion of wearing black coats for evening dress. Next came *The Disowned,* published in December 1828, in which Bulwer fictionalized scenes from his life among the gypsies in 1824 as well as from his adventures in France the following year. His fourth novel, *Devereux,* appeared in June 1829 and described events set in the eighteenth century during Queen Anne's reign. But his debut as a historical novelist proved disappointing as he had not yet fully mastered the genre.

In August 1830 Bulwer published *Paul Clifford,* his first Newgate crime novel, which called for reforms in the judicial system. During 1831 he wrote *The Siamese Twins,* a long satirical poem about life in modern London, and brought out an edition of *Collected Poems.* His psychological crime thriller, *Eugene Aram* (1832), raised a chorus of abuse from the critics who objected to a novel with a murderer as its hero. In *Godolphin,* published in 1833, Bulwer again took fashionable life as his subject, introducing an occult theme in the novel's subplot that foreshadowed his great occult thrillers of the next three decades. The same year his two-volume *England and the English* appeared, in which he masterfully dissected and analyzed English social manners of the last thirty years. In it he demonstrated that he fully understood the zeitgeist of the postwar years, and he correctly predicted what industrial and democratic England would be like in the coming decades. Next to R. H. Horne's *The New Spirit of the Age* (1844), Bulwer's book provides an impressive record of the regency and early Victorian ages.

Also in 1833 Bulwer's metaphysical fantasy, *The Pilgrims of the Rhine,* was printed; it represents his memorial to the death of his first love at Ealing. Following a trip with Rosina to Italy during 1833–34, Bulwer renewed his interest in the historical romance. In *The Last Days of Pompeii* (1834)—his most popular novel—and in *Rienzi* (1835), he wrote about both ancient and medieval Italy during periods of great social transformation. He effectively displayed his wide reading of ancient history in his nonfiction study *Athens, Its Rise and Fall* (1837), which came out in two volumes. The same year Bulwer published *Ernest Maltravers,* a novel in which he skillfully blended metaphysics and fashionable life. With its sequel, *Alice* (1838), he produced one of the best novels of self-education before Charles Dickens's *David Copperfield* (1849–50). *Maltravers* and *Alice* combine to make a single, unified novel, containing important autobiographical insights about Bulwer and his views on authorship. In *Maltravers* the hero complains that "few persons understand and forbear with and pity [the author]," who "sells his health and youth to a rugged task master."[19] Reflecting Bulwer's overwork and weariness are *Leila; or, The Siege of Granada* and *Calderon the Courtier* (1838). Set in Spain during the fifteenth century, they are merely hastily constructed sensational potboilers.

His writings between 1827 and 1838 proved greatly popular with the public, who rightly saw Bulwer as a rising star among the new generation of novelists. But he paid a heavy price for literary success, as the constant need to get a living by his pen led to the failure of his marriage.

Bulwer's intense labor, his grandson observed, could not be sustained without some sacrifice to health and domestic happiness. He noted that Bulwer "always [fought] against time, every hindrance and interruption was a provocation, and petty household worries were magnified into serious grievances."[20] In the hectic, fevered life he led, Rosina had no place. When not actually writing or reading in preparation for writing, Bulwer, his grandson noted, sought relaxation and intellectual stimulation in the society of other writers and close friends who broke the monotony of his constant literary drudgery. While he provided his wife with every luxury and comfort, Bulwer deprived Rosina of his own companionship and personal sympathy. He frequently became irritable, breaking out into violent fits of temper followed by self-reproach and hasty reconciliations.[21] According to Mary Greene, who visited the couple frequently, Bulwer seemed "like a man who had been flayed, and is sore all over."[22] However, Rosina refused to suffer such behavior calmly; as egotistical as Bulwer, she desired to be amused and hungered for attention to be paid her by reason of her own beauty and talents. Rosina did not intend to be relegated to being merely the wife of a rising literary star.[23]

Given such difficulties, the marriage fell apart during their trip to Italy in 1833. While Bulwer absorbed himself in research for his two Italian historical romances, Rosina found a romantic substitute in a Neapolitan prince who courted, praised, and flattered her. Enraged by jealousy, Bulwer upbraided Rosina for her infidelity; she accused him of neglect, claiming he no longer cared for her. Bulwer ordered his wife to break off the attachment and return immediately with him to England. The journey home in 1834 was a "protracted nightmare of mutual recriminations, and soon after their return they decided to live apart for a time."[24] For the next two years they sought a reconciliation, but each attempt resulted in new quarrels, leading to a final estrangement. In April 1836 Rosina received a deed of judicial separation; Bulwer gave her custody of their two children and an income for their maintenance.[25] To fill the void in his private life, Bulwer turned to further literary work and a career in Parliament.

Radical Politician and Member of Parliament

As a Whig-Liberal committed to political reform, Bulwer entered Parliament in May 1831, representing the rural borough of St. Ives in Huntingdonshire. He supported Lord John Russell's proposed reform bill, giving his maiden speech in the House of Commons on the second night of the debate. When the bill passed by a majority of 109, the Lords in the upper house rejected it, leading to a new election. The new Parliament, one determined to widen the franchise and correct longstanding electoral abuses, finally passed the Reform Bill, a victory accepted in the Lords and reluctantly assented to by the king on 7 June 1832. Bulwer's constituency at St. Ives was one of those swept away by the Reform Act, and he stood for election at Lincoln, returning to Parliament the following session.

In his first stint in the House of Commons (1831–41), Bulwer actively supported numerous legislative reforms—including breaking the monopoly on patented theaters, liberalizing dramatic censorship, increasing the protection against literary piracy, reducing stamp taxes on newspapers and magazines, and seeking financial support for indigent writers. He attended the Commons regularly, speaking occasionally on issues he felt needed public discussion. During his tenure in the Commons, he achieved two outstanding successes: his pamphlet entitled *Letter to a Late Cabinet Minister on the Present Crisis* (1834) and his support for the immediate abolition of Negro apprenticeship in the West Indian colonies (1838).

His pamphlet came in response to a Tory attempt to regain office in 1834. The public expected Lord Melbourne's Whig government to carry out immediate, widespread social reforms. When it did not, general dissatisfaction set in, which the king and the Tories misread as a general reaction against reform. The king used the death of Lord Spencer as a pretext to get rid of the Whig government.

Lord Althorpe, Spencer's son and the Whig chancellor of the exchequer, was elevated to the House of Lords, leaving a vacancy in the government. Pretending Althorpe could not be replaced, the king informed Lord Melbourne in November 1834 that he no longer enjoyed his confidence and that his ministry should resign. The ultraconservative duke of Wellington formed a caretaker government but advised the king to summon Sir Robert Peel to assemble an anti-reform Tory administration. The duke hoped that Peel would seem moderate enough to the Whigs to attract a few genuine reformers and convince the public that the Tories embraced reform.

Bulwer and the other Whigs, however, recognized that a Peel government would be a bad substitute and that it was essential to return the Whigs to office at the next general election. To achieve this aim, Bulwer set to work to expose the Tory's political strategy in his *Letter to a Late Minister on the Present Crisis,* written in only two days. Saunders and Otley published it on 21 November 1834, and it proved an immediate political success, running to twenty-one editions in six weeks. It was quoted at length in many leading papers. Whig candidates used it as the basis of their election speeches, which contributed to a Whig victory at the polls and their return to office. In a letter to his friend John Forster, Bulwer said that more than twelve Commons members told him that they owed their seats to his pamphlet. Bulwer won reelection, and in appreciation for his services Lord Melbourne offered him a minor post in the new Whig government, which he declined to accept.[26]

In his pamphlet Bulwer displayed his astute powers as a partisan politician, accurately reading the temper of the times. His support in May 1838 for Sir Eardley Wilmot's resolution to abolish Negro apprenticeship in the West Indian colonies illustrated his humanity and political idealism. Outright slavery in the West Indian colonies had been abolished in 1833, but the original legislation provided a twelve-year transition period during which the emancipated slaves were required to work for their former owners as apprentices with the rights of free men. However, the apprentice system proved wholly unsatisfactory, for during the five years following abolition, the condition of the Negroes was little better than before emancipation. Bulwer felt that the West Indian planters had failed to keep faith with the government, and he spoke out in the Commons, exposing the abuses of the apprenticeship system and calling for the total emancipation of Negro workers. In his speech—which political reformer Daniel O'Connell thought one of the best ever heard in the Commons—he attacked the apprenticeship system, labeling it tyranny made legal. He urged his colleagues not to break faith with justice or humanity, warning them that any attempt to relax or mitigate slavery would be both hopeless and absurd. There is, he told the Commons, "something holier than the gratification of party triumph and political ambition" and it lies "in the applause of . . . conscience, and in those blessings" of "the victims of human avarice and pride."[27] The vote immediately followed Bulwer's speech, and Wilmot's resolution won 96 to 93. Afterward three Commons members told Bulwer that they had intended to vote against the resolution but had been converted by his speech.[28]

During the 1830s Bulwer belonged to Lord Durham's group of philosophical radicals, a faction of ardent political reformers in the Whig left. At no time did Bulwer ever join the innermost circle of the Whig political aristocracy, nor was he a strong party man. Like the politicians in his novels, he prized his political independence, voting for the issue rather than the man or party. He corresponded frequently with John Stuart Mill and with the radical philosopher William Godwin; both saw him as an advanced reformer sympathetic to their own views. In *Pelham* and the early novels following it, Bulwer dramatized his commitment to Benthamite reforms, calling for the removal of legislation that impeded the creation of a rational and humane society. Godwin's influence can be found in *Paul Clifford,* where Bulwer lashed out against class legislation and age-old abuses in the penal laws. His only political allegiance was to Lord Durham, who at one time sought to create a new political party to act as the vanguard of liberal reform. But when Durham accepted appointment as British ambassador to St. Petersburg, Bulwer's interest in politics diminished, and he aired his political opinions in his novels rather than in the House of Commons. In 1841 Bulwer resigned his seat in Parliament and retired from active political life. He remained outside the Commons for eleven years, returning to it in 1852 as a political conservative and supporter of his friend Benjamin Disraeli. During his absence from the Commons, Bulwer again turned to authorship, gaining great success as a novelist and playwright.

The Middle Years: Dramatist and Novelist

Few Victorian novelists succeeded in the theater as playwrights. Bulwer was the exception to the rule, as he wrote over a dozen plays, half of them enjoying public success in London and provincial theaters. Early in his career he wrote a play about Oliver Cromwell, which actor-manager W. C. Macready asked to read. Macready judged it unsuitable for the stage, however, and it was never performed or published. But Macready encouraged Bulwer's dramatic aspirations, and on 4 January 1837, he staged a play by Bulwer called *The Duchess de la Valliere*. It told the story of a courtier in the days of Louis XIV and her tragic love for a knightly soldier. The audience heartily approved of the play the first night, but succeeding audiences failed to sustain this verdict. It was withdrawn from performance several days later.

Even though Macready rejected his first play and audiences disapproved of his second, Bulwer continued his interest in writing for the stage. His historical drama, *The Lady of Lyons,* opened on 15 February 1838 at Covent Garden under Macready's direction. Treating life in revolutionary France during the Directory (1795–99), the play focuses on the breakdown of class barriers and the rise of a middle class of talent and wealth. The subject appealed to London audiences who judged it a complete dramatic success.

Equally successful was *Richelieu,* a five-act play in blank verse, staged on 7 March 1839 at Covent Garden, where it was well received by the public. Such success encouraged Bulwer to write another play, *The Sea Captain,* which ran several weeks at the Haymarket theater in October 1839. Thackeray, who disliked the play, bitterly attacked it in his satirical *Yellowplush Papers.* Bulwer altered the play, and it reappeared in 1868 under the title *The Rightful Heir.* Of all Bulwer's plays, none proved more popular and durable than his comedy *Money,* which first played at the Haymarket on 8 December 1840 and continued to run until May 1841. Dickens saw it and wrote Bulwer on 12 December 1841 to congratulate him on its brilliant success. So popular did this drawing-room comedy become that it was selected on 17 May 1911 to be performed at Drury Lane in honor of Wilhelm II's visit to England for the coronation of King George V. Of Bulwer's other plays—*Not So Bad as We Seem* (1851), *Walpole* (1869), and *Darnley* (1882)—only the first ranks with *The Lady of Lyons, Richelieu,* and *Money* as his best dramatic work. These four plays continued to run in provincial theaters throughout the rest of the century. But Macready's retirement from the theater ended Bulwer's incentive to write for the stage. His own retirement from Parliament in 1841 allowed him greater leisure to write, and he concentrated on creating novels, which became the main work of his life after 1841.

During the 1840s Bulwer published some of his best novels, works that earned him a reputation as an important novelist but subjected him to frequent attack by hostile critics at *Fraser's Magazine*. *Night and Morning,* his metaphysical crime novel, came out in 1841 to a chorus of critical outcry against its comparison of fashionable vice and ungenteel crime. Far different in subject was *Zanoni* (1842), Bulwer's first full-length metaphysical novel of the occult. It proved popular but puzzling to contemporary readers, who failed to recognize its underlying Christian thesis. In 1834 he returned to the historical novel with *The Last of the Barons,* which demonstrated his mastery of the genre and earned him the respect of contemporary historians for his careful reconstruction of the era of Warwick and Edward IV. *Lucretia* (1846) was Bulwer's last Newgate crime novel, a book portraying the brutal crimes of real-life poisoner Thomas Wainewright and his wife. Periodical critics protested *Lucretia* because it dwelled so heavily on dark crimes and moral transgressions. Shocked by the critics, Bulwer contemplated retiring from authorship but decided instead to publish a defense of his crime fiction in a pamphlet called *A Word to the Public* (1847).

Critical opposition to his crime novels played some part in Bulwer's decision to abandon Newgate fiction. Beginning with *Harold* (1848), he pursued less sensational subjects. A dramatization of the events leading to the Battle of Hastings in 1066, *Harold* was Bulwer's last completed historical novel—and certainly his best work in the genre, earning him the praise of Lord Macaulay and other contemporary historians. *The Caxtons* (1850) saw Bulwer's return to domestic fiction, a genre he had not worked in since the early 1830s. Set in contemporary England, it fictionalized his theories about comedy, which had their origin in his play *Money* (1840). With *The Caxtons* and its two successors in the series—*My Novel* (1853) and *What Will He Do with It?* (1858)—Bulwer successfully competed with Anthony Trollope and George Eliot as a novelist of domestic life. All three Caxton novels won the affection of the public, and through them Bulwer reached a wider audience than ever before.

Yet such popular acclaim failed to please him, and he returned to
Parliament to espouse his recently acquired conservative beliefs.

Return to Parliament and Cabinet Minister

The years of his absence from the House of Commons gradually
brought about a significant change in Bulwer's political philosophy.
He returned to the Commons as a Conservative in the general election of 1852, sitting this time for Hertfordshire. In his pamphlet
Letters to John Bull (1851), Bulwer explained the sources of his
conversion from liberal to conservative beliefs. The death of his
mother in 1843, his inheritance of her property at Knebworth, his
lack of strong party ties, his detached study of political issues, his
fear of unrest on the continent, and his growing friendship with
Benjamin Disraeli all played a part in his move to the right.

Two circumstances directly contributed to Bulwer's new political
allegiance. He broke with the Liberals over the repeal of the Corn
Laws, and the extreme laissez-faire doctrines embraced by the Manchester (Cobdenite) school greatly angered him. As a result of the
industrial revolution, middle-class manufacturers came to power,
men whose prosperity arose from free trade rather than from agricultural protection.[29] All the sympathies that had made Bulwer an
ardent reformer in his earlier years, his grandson observed, "were
now in revolt against the selfishness of this new commercial school,
which cared nothing for the sufferings of the working population
that produced their wealth, and which opposed all attempts of the
State to intervene for their protection."[30] In 1848 Bulwer complained to John Forster that the great manufacturers were "wretched
money spiders, who would sell England for 1*s*. 6*d*."[31] Given his
idealism, Bulwer felt more comfortable with Disraeli's Tory democracy than with the laissez-faire ideology of the Liberal party,
and his idealism provided the bridge by which he passed over to
the Conservative party.[32]

Back in Parliament, Bulwer took an active part in debating the
issues of the day. He supported the government during the Crimean
War, taking a pro-war, anti-Russian stance. In addition he advo-
cated administrative reform and the introduction of competitive
examinations in 1855, denounced the treatment of China following
the Arrow dispute in 1857, and opposed the abolition of the East
India Company in 1857, fearing it would open Indian policy to

parliamentary intrigue. But his greatest personal success in the Commons came in 1855, when Bulwer induced the government to abolish the stamp duties on newspapers, which he often referred to as a tax upon knowledge. His interest in this issue dated to 1835, when he first fought against any form of government control over the publication and distribution of printed materials.

Following the fall of Lord Palmerston's government in 1858, Lord Derby and the Conservatives formed an administration, and Bulwer accepted the post of secretary of state for the colonies in the new government.[33] Bulwer's tenure of office was short, lasting little over a year (1858–59), yet as a cabinet minister he energetically carried out the functions of his office. He was chiefly concerned with policy for Australia and Canada, and today in both these colonies flourishing towns bear his name. Bulwer's concern in Australia was to draw up a plan for the administrative separation of Queensland from New South Wales and to secure the appointment of Sir George Bowen as governor of the new colony. In Canada Bulwer supervised the incorporation of British Columbia as a new colony on the North American continent—the most important act of his administration. On 8 July 1858 he introduced a bill to establish the Crown's rights to the gold discovered in the Fraser River district and to preserve order and protect life and property among the new settlers attracted to the area by the discovery of gold. The bill empowered the Crown to make laws for the district for five years and provided for a representative government at the end of that period. The bill's passage in the Commons led to the establishment of the new colony and the settlement of one of the richest districts in Canada. Other activities undertaken by Bulwer included the passage of the Encumbered Estates Bill for the West Indian colonies, the settlement of a dispute with France over the exchange of Portendio for Albuda, and the dispatch of Gladstone to the Ionian Islands to determine whether they should be united to Greece or kept under a British protectorate.[34]

At the end of 1858 Bulwer suffered a physical breakdown, arising from overwork and difficulties with his wife, who had long embarrassed him in public after their separation in 1836. She wrote several novels in which she accused him of the most vile conduct toward her. Throughout the early 1840s Lady Bulwer remained abroad but returned home in 1847 intent on blackmailing her ex-husband for a larger allowance. To accomplish her aim, she addressed obscene letters to Bulwer at his residence, club, and Commons office, sending as many as twenty in one day.

Lady Bulwer also dispatched similar letters to her husband's friends, including Lord Lyndhurst, Sir Francis Doyle, John Forster, Charles Dickens, and Benjamin Disraeli. In 1851 she wrote the duke of Devonshire on the occasion of the appearance of Bulwer's play at Devonshire House in aid of the Guild of Literature, threatening to enter the house in disguise, pelt Queen Victoria with rotten eggs, and expose the queen as the cold-blooded murderess of Lady Flora Hastings. The duke employed detective police to guard against such outrages. On 8 June 1858 Lady Bulwer attacked her husband in public while he addressed his constituents at Hertford during the 1858 elections. She mounted the platform and harangued the crowd, exclaiming, "How can the people of England submit to have such a man at the head of the Colonies, who ought to have been in the Colonies as a transport [transported felon] long ago."[35]

After securing medical advice about his wife, Bulwer arranged her removal to Inverness Lodge on 23 June 1858 as a person of unsound mind, on the authority of a certificate signed by two physicians who had previously interviewed Lady Bulwer. Detained three weeks, Lady Bulwer and her misfortune became a matter taken up by the London and provincial press. Most of the articles severely criticized the action of the colonial secretary, and Bulwer's colleagues in the government feared a sensational scandal. Fortunately the incident was kept out of the courts when Bulwer's son, Robert, offered to take his mother abroad if she could be released. Both parents welcomed the suggestion, and she left Inverness Lodge for Bordeaux on 17 July with her son and a female attendant. After several months abroad, Lady Bulwer returned to England, where she maintained an uneasy peace with her ex-husband for the remainder of their lives. She outlived Bulwer, dying at Upper Sydenham on 12 March 1882 at the age of eighty.[36]

On 16 December 1858 Bulwer wrote his chief, Lord Derby, submitting his resignation from the cabinet for reasons of ill health. But Derby asked him to remain through the new year; he was preparing his reform bill and wished no rumors of dissension in the cabinet to undermine its presentation. Bulwer complied, and when Disraeli introduced the bill in the Commons on 28 February 1859, Bulwer spoke in its support on the second night of debate. At the conclusion of the debate on 31 March 1859, Derby's government resigned, though Bulwer continued in office until a replacement could be found from the new government. He retained his seat in the Commons until 1866, when he was raised to the peerage and elevated to the House of Lords as Baron Lytton of Knebworth. While he followed politics throughout the rest of his life, his interests once again turned to literature. His grandson noted that Bulwer essentially belonged to an aristocratic age, and the end of his political career coincided with the close of that age.[37] In his dislike of the Cobdenites, his fear of unsettling ideas, and his anger at Corn Law repeal, Bulwer reflected the views of his own social class, the rural landowning gentry.

Late Writings and Last Years

Freed from his political duties, Bulwer concentrated once more on novel writing and produced some of his best work at the close of his career. He abandoned fictional realism and with the publication of *A Strange Story* (1862) created an exciting metaphysical novel with an occult theme, taking Darwinism to task by reaffirming traditional Christian values. His *Caxtoniana* essays followed in 1863, containing a collection of short articles published during the preceding two decades on a great variety of topics, ranging from the clairvoyance of the artistic imagination to the art of comedy.

The Lost Tales of Miletus, a book of poems, appeared in 1866, followed by a rhymed comic play, *Walpole; or, Every Man Has His Price* (1869). Bulwer's interest in classical writers is reflected in his translation of *The Odes and Epodes of Horace,* also printed in 1869. His satirical dystopia, *The Coming Race,* came out anonymously in 1871, receiving wide public attention and general critical approval. It contained his most forthright attack to date on what he believed to be the false democratic spirit of the age. In 1873, the year of his death, Bulwer's metaphysical romance, *Kenelm Chillingly* appeared, featuring an attack on conservative-inspired political reforms and accusing Disraeli of being too forward in his reforming zeal in Parliament. After his death, Bulwer's antirevolutionary epic novel, *The Parisians,* came out in 1873, assailing French intellectuals and radical politicians for undermining civilization with their advanced ideas. In 1876 Bulwer's son published *Pausanias the Spartan,* an unfinished historical novel of some promise. For this book, Robert Lytton had collaborated with Bulwer's old college friend, the classical scholar Benjamin Hall Kennedy, to piece together the late author's notes into a coherent narrative.

On the whole Bulwer's last years were singularly lonely, for neither in literature nor in politics did he belong to any intimate set. He went little into society, living alone part of the year at his country home of Knebworth and part of the year on the continent, where he took the waters to restore his failing health. His chief literary friends were the editor and critic John Forster and Charles Dickens; his only close political friend was Benjamin Disraeli. Had his daughter lived—she died of typhoid fever in 1848—she might have provided Bulwer with the female companionship he so desperately missed after his separation from Lady Bulwer. While he and his son Robert became close in later years, Robert's diplomatic assignments abroad kept them apart for long intervals. Both corresponded frequently, candidly discussing public and private matters, their common interest in poetry bringing them closer as the years advanced. Bulwer took great pride in his son's career as a poet, and he advised Robert, who wrote under the name of Owen Meredith, on many of the verses he undertook to publish. Toward the close of his life, Bulwer lost his hearing, which made socializing difficult for a proud man who was shy and reserved in public. His loss made attending the proceedings of the House of Lords difficult, too; yet he occasionally sat in the Lords for important debates such as the vote on the Second Reform Bill (1867), about which he entertained some reservations, seeing it as a great leap in the dark.

Bulwer's last years were quiet ones, during which he received recognition for his contributions to literature. Following the vacancy created by Lord Derby's death (1869), he was offered and accepted the Order of St. Michael and St. George on 15 January 1870. Earlier he had been given an honorary LL.D. from Oxford University and been elected Lord Rector of Glasgow University in 1856 and 1858, the only Englishman upon whom the honor had been twice conferred. In 1862 he received an offer of the throne of Greece, left vacant by the abdication of King Otho, an offer also made to Gladstone and Lord Stanley. Bulwer humorously wrote to his son that he had "thrown icewater" on the proposal; it appeared far from alluring as Greece had little revenue and "seemed head over ears in debt." All, he observed, looked "dismal beside the calm Academe of Knebworth."[38]

Bulwer's last months were probably his happiest. Robert Lytton and his wife stayed with Bulwer at Torquay during November and December 1872, visiting while he labored over the last chapters of *Kenelm Chillingly*. After their departure on 4 January 1873, Bulwer fell ill, complaining of great pain and violent noises in both ears. Doctors attended him and succeeded in providing him with some relief, but the pains on the right side of his face and neck gradually increased. A few days later he lost his sight and his mind began to wander. During the night of 17 January, he suffered a series of epileptic fits and convulsions, dying in his sleep on 18 January 1873. The cause of his death proved to be an inflammation of the membranes of the brain, resulting from an ear disease from which he had suffered for many years.[39]

Funeral services for Bulwer took place on 25 January 1873, and on 2 February Professor Jowett preached a funeral sermon at Westminster Abbey, where Bulwer was buried in the chapel of St. Edmund's near the Poets' Corner. His son received many letters of sympathy, including expressions of admiration for Bulwer from Disraeli, Gladstone, John Morley, John Forster, and Robert Browning.

During his lifetime Bulwer may have been the most widely read novelist next to Dickens. He was essentially an intellectual writer and not a popular storyteller. Most of his novels abound in evidence of a serious, scholarly, and intellectual mind, revealing a man of wide reading, deep knowledge, and clear insight into human character. Anthony Trollope, one of his contemporaries, recognized this quality in his writings. In his *Autobiography* he says of Bulwer that he "was a man of very great parts. Better educated than either [Thackeray or Dickens], he was always able to use his erudition, and he thus produced novels from which very much not only may be, but must be, gleaned by his readers. . . . He had read extensively, and was always apt to give his readers the benefit of what he knew. The result has been that very much more than amusement may be obtained from Bulwer's novels."[40] Bulwer's fiction, composed in a dozen different literary genres, is not merely popular entertainment but rather work of aesthetic seriousness. His books speak today because of their great variety and their high level of excellence.

Chapter Two
Bulwer's Byronic Apprenticeship and His Early Novels, 1820–29

Bulwer's romantic relationships—the Ealing affair of 1820 and his infatuation with Lady Caroline Lamb at Brocket Park in 1824—were the most important extraliterary sources shaping his apprentice writings. These incidents generated themes that informed his earliest works and were recurring motifs throughout his long writing career. In particular, the lost love of a woman Bulwer deemed nearly perfect (Lucy D—— at Ealing) and his dissatisfaction with a relationship ruled by gratified vanity rather than heartfelt sympathy (Lady Lamb) were themes central to his earliest writings. These writings, constituting his period of apprenticeship, can be divided into two phases. The first, which includes his juvenilia, Cambridge, and nonprofessional writing, spans the period 1820–26. It begins with the publication of his first verse collection, *Ismael,* and ends with the work done on the unfinished novella "Glenallan." The second phase, his first two years as a full-time author, dates from the publication of *Falkland* in 1827 to the appearance of *Devereux* in 1829. This nine-year apprenticeship was characterized by a steady movement away from Byronism toward the development, by 1828, of his own voice as a novelist. During this period Bulwer experimented with occasional and dramatic verse, topical essays, historical writing, and two contrasting approaches to the novel already evolving from a fairly well defined aesthetic about the art of fiction. Such experimentation would yield many successful mature works, not a few based on these early writings.

Of immediate interest, however, is the scope and direction taken in Bulwer's apprentice writings. At the earliest stage he thought of himself primarily as a poet, or at least a potential poet. But though he published four volumes of verse before 1827, he soon came to the conclusion that his real literary gifts were best suited for the novel.

Lord Byron's death in 1824, Bulwer's vows at Ealing to commit his artistic energies to the external world, and several publishing opportunities for his prose fiction after 1826 confirmed Bulwer in his turn from poetry to novel writing. Evidence of this shift can be seen in the growing number of tales and novellas he wrote between 1823 and 1826. These stories, many Byronic in subject and style, reflect Bulwer's great emotional and artistic debt to Byron. In them, Bulwer worked to synthesize all the elements and conventions found in the Byron cult. He achieved such a synthesis in his first novel, *Falkland*. Aside from being the best example of Byronic fiction of the period, *Falkland*'s real significance was that it exorcised Byron's hold over Bulwer's imagination and freed him to pursue different subjects and to use other literary styles. Bulwer's work at the close of his apprenticeship—*Pelham, The Disowned, Greville,* and *Devereux*—represented a movement forward to work in the silver-fork, bildungsroman, metaphysical, and historical costume-romance genres. Except for *Falkland* and *Pelham,* however, Bulwer's earliest prose works are not well known. A brief examination of the more significant of them serves to shed some light on his development as a novelist and as an influential Victorian man of letters.

Early Unpublished Apprenticeship Novels: "Mortimer," "De Lindsay," "Linda," and "Glenallan"

Bulwer's prose-fiction apprenticeship begins in 1825 with a tale called "Mortimer; or, The Memoirs of a Gentleman," which after 1826 was expanded into *Pelham* (1828). "Mortimer" is a bright, cynical story that affects a tone of unscrupulous levity to show how society can corrupt a young man of fashion. "Mortimer" and the original 1824 sketch of *Falkland* represent parallel, contrasting experiments in fictional theory. Bulwer was working out two approaches to fiction—what he referred to in his *Autobiography* as the impassioned and somber and the light and sportive styles. In the first Bulwer worked to update traditional gothic-romance conventions by infusing them with Byronic themes. By 1830 such experiments evolved into Bulwer's Newgate and urban crime novels; later the same strain shaped his occult and supernatural fiction. The contrasting light and sportive approach led to his silver-fork satires and, by the late 1840s, became the source for his Caxton domestic novel series. A direct by-product of this early experimentation was "De Lindsay," a novella drawn in the impassioned and somber style. Written in 1825, it was a Byronic thriller superimposed over the older sentimental romance genre. "De Lindsay" also has important autobiographical significance as it fictionalized both Bulwer's Ealing and Brocket Park affairs.

Among other literary projects started in 1825 was a three-volume novel called "Linda, A Romance," which was never finished. Set in Germany, both its subject and its style are mystical. Also in 1825, Bulwer wrote a short, untitled tale based on the Rosicrucian Brotherhood. This tale is significant because it contained many of the themes Bulwer later employed in *Zicci* (1838), which he finally recast as the novel *Zanoni* in 1842. Another fragment from this period was the prose tale "Glenallan" (1826), set in Ireland at Castle Tyrone. It describes the rivalries between two cousins named Redmon and Ruthven Glenallan. "Glenallan" is not developed beyond six chapters; however, the tale was recast in verse with only slight name and plot changes and titled *O'Neill; or, The Rebel*. It is a long dramatic poem filled with what Bulwer termed rebels, banshees, and scaffolds. *O'Neill* was published by Henry Colburn in June 1827.[1]

Early Published Novels, 1827–29: *Falkland* as Bulwer Byronized

Falkland, Bulwer's first published novel, was brought out anonymously in one volume by Henry Colburn in March 1827. In an 1826 letter to his fiancée, Rosina Wheeler, Bulwer claimed that he published *Falkland* "to open some field for the introduction of [his] Poetry. . . . Now if *Falkland* succeeds at all, it will do so sufficiently to obtain a reading for 'Poems.' "[2] Bulwer was dissatisfied with the final form of *Falkland,* which Colburn accepted for publication. He thought it fell "very far short of the plan I had intended to execute."[3] His friend Mary Greene was disappointed in the book, calling it "horrid," and condemning it for its "bad sentiments" and "infamous morals."[4] Bulwer's mother praised *Falkland* as a remarkable achievement for someone so young, but she too objected to its unchristian stance—especially the ending in which the hero reflects so little of the Christian Spirit. In sum, *Falkland* impressed its few readers as a morally loose book, an opinion later amplified in the general indictment of Bulwer as an immoral and dangerous writer.[5]

Falkland provides the reader with a sustained inside view of the hidden dreams, the inner inconsistencies, and the misdirected energies of the novel's two central characters as they actively pursue their own self-destruction. Originally a man of action, Falkland grows tired of the external world, which to him is servility knit to arrogance and meanness tied to ostentation. A love of extremes rules his character: he alternates between restless action and idle reflection, between dislike of individuals and love for mankind, and between sensual indulgence and ascetic celibacy. For Falkland there is no middle ground between ecstasy and dark dejection; he purposely eschews moderation and tempered emotions. He has a blighted past that combines seduction with callous, unforgivable conduct to his victims. In short, Falkland is a Byronic dark hero who fools himself into believing that the losses of the heart can be repaired by the experiences of the mind.

Emily Mandeville is beautiful, quick in feeling, regular in temper, and gay—less from levity than from the first spring tide of a heart yet to be sad. She is pure, innocent, and deeply religious, with an admiration for the good and a contempt for whatever is mean and worthless. As a conventionally married woman, Emily is obedient to the usages of society. She is centered in home, husband, and her child. Her husband, John, has an ascetic bent of character, and is not much above the average man in temperament or talent. He is rather a "slow horse" for such a young wife. When separated from Emily, Mandeville can think of nothing more romantic than to send her a volume on political economy to read together with two of his corrected parliamentary speeches. Emily is a representative of bland smoothness, implying the triumph of civilization over all the interesting unevenness and passion of nature. Married before she knew herself to a man impossible to love, Emily's only escape from misery is in the dormancy of feeling. Yet feeling is awakened by the birth of her son, Henry. With this event, deep, hidden springs of emotion surface in Emily.

Falkland and Emily meet, and after their first formal introduction, Emily is left with Falkland's "low soft voice [ringing] in her ear, like the music of an indistinct and half-remembered dream."[6] What follows is a pattern of romantic advance and retreat on Emily's part, as she is tempted to claim the love she has never known but clings to the social sureties she needs. Falkland also participates in this pattern. He veers between bold assertion to claim his ideal passion and guilt-stricken inaction. Finally Falkland presses forward and openly woos Emily, telling her that "adultery of the heart is no less a crime than that of the deed" (71). Encouraging her to elope with him, Falkland claims that "if you loved like me, you would feel it was something of pride—of triumph to dare all things, even crime" (71). Eventually, they consummate their union and later are exposed. Mandeville's accusations cause Emily to burst a blood vessel and die. Falkland experiences remorse, suffering, repentance, and a sense of doom as he is haunted by guilty dreams—visions of fiery hells, serpents, and Emily's accusing face. He escapes to Spain to fight on the Constitutionalist side in the revolution, not motivated by high hopes and chivalry but merely seeking excitement and forgetfulness—reversing his political idealism through his guilty escape into self-pity. Betrayed by an enemy in Spain, Falkland is murdered and dies at exactly half past midnight (the hour of Emily's death) with a ringlet of her hair pressed to his breast.

Bulwer's achievement in *Falkland,* aside from purging both his youthful egotism and his painful memories of unrequited love, is his skillful blending of established literary genres and conventions. He took his own fanciful view of himself as an arch-seducer of the age and united it with the cult of Byron, adding liberal portions of romanticism and gothicism—elements taken from Wordsworth, Scott, Rousseau, Radcliffe, Monk Lewis, Godwin, and Maturin. Bulwer's use of multiple literary formulas—such as gothic, Byronic, silver-fork, and adventure patterns—is a method of construction he was to employ throughout his writing career; it became a compositional trademark and an authorial signature. He is also effective in his use of gothic landscape to generate tone, to sustain atmosphere, and to achieve heightened dramatic effect. The novel's controlling themes—self-destructive egoism, yearning for human sympathy, criticism of the ritualistic forms in conventional society, idealistic demands for benevolence and political freedom, and conflicts between the public and the private self—are central motifs in Bulwer's early writings, and they recur and give coherence to many of his works published after *Falkland.*

Pelham as the Education of a Benthamite Hero

Bulwer's next novel, *Pelham, or, The Adventures of a Gentleman,* was published anonymously by Henry Colburn in three volumes on

10 May 1828. It was based on Bulwer's earlier sketch, "Mortimer; or, The Memoirs of a Gentleman," written in 1825 to illustrate how worldliness can corrupt character. Bulwer altered this thesis in the 1827 revision in order to show how character can be redeemed through the proper use of worldly experience, growing gradually wiser by learning from his youthful foibles. Bulwer planned *Pelham* around the idea that the lessons of society do not necessarily corrupt. But he never intended *Pelham* to be primarily a novel of society in the silver-fork tradition. He later wrote: "Had I imagined . . . that *Pelham* would be considered a fashionable novel, I would have burnt every page of it. For I understand by the term 'fashionable novel' a description of things, and I intended *Pelham* for a description of *persons*. It was not my aim to paint drawing-rooms, but to paint the people in them—their characters and humors."[7]

Bulwer received £500 for the copyright after a period of uncertain negotiations with Henry Colburn and his staff. Colburn's chief reader, Shoberl, strongly advised him not to publish *Pelham,* for he thought it utterly worthless.[8] But Colburn asked the opinion of his second reader, Charles Ollier, who praised the manuscript and later told Bulwer that "nothing has come out to equal it since [Thomas Hope's novel] *Anastasius* [1819]. . . . It will succeed greatly."[9] Colburn read the manuscript and declared to his staff that it would be the smash of the season. Once published, *Pelham* was a sleeper for the first two months, generating little interest. Aside from flattering notices placed by Colburn in the *Literary Gazette,* the *Examiner,* and the *Atlas,* it was received by the critics with either indifference or abuse. But after the third month of publication, *Pelham* caught on and soon fulfilled Colburn's enthusiastic predictions—it became the book of the season. It sold so well that Colburn sent a second £500 check following the sixth edition in recognition of the author's moral claim to a larger share of the profits.[10]

Public enthusiasm for *Pelham* was overwhelming; it soon became the talk of London. There were imitations and parodies, including a series that ran in the *Age* from 11 to 18 October 1829. The novel even effected a change in fashionable dress. Up to that time men had worn formal evening coats of many different colors, but Bulwer's novel made black the only acceptable shade for evening wear. *Pelham* was translated into German, Spanish, Italian, and French, generating as much interest abroad as at home. In fact, *Pelham* was consulted as an index to English manners by its foreign readers.

The very name Pelham, for example, came to mean a rather fast young man. An anonymous French reviewer in the *Revue des Deux Mondes* claimed that *Pelham* "had become a text-book about English society in all the salons, cafes, and the clubs of Paris."[11]

If *Falkland* focuses on the Byronic dark side of the self, *Pelham*, its artistic complement, celebrates in a light and witty style the proper accommodation of the self to the external world. All of Bulwer's complementary subordinate formula patterns—silver-fork satire; political novel; Pierce Egan–like tour of turf and London low-life; sensational story of Byronic seduction, rape, revenge, and guilty remorse; detective quest; and story of separated lovers—are united by a controlling bildungsroman design. This pattern features a hero who grows up in the country and is a child of some sensibility. He finds constraints, both social and intellectual, upon his free imagination. Often his family is hostile to his flights of fancy; his parents are both antagonistic to his ambitions and quite impervious to the new ideas he gains from unprescribed reading. Usually his schooling, if not totally inadequate, is frustrating in not suggesting options available in his present setting. The hero leaves home and goes to the city (most often London), where his real education begins. Such an education is based on direct experience of urban life and involvement in at least two love affairs, one debasing, the other exalting. The latter affair forces the hero to reappraise his personal values, and after much painful soul-searching, he decides how best to accommodate himself to the modern world. In this process the hero leaves his adolescence behind and enters into maturity. Initiation complete, he may revisit his old home to demonstrate the degree of success or wisdom of his choice.[12]

The bildungsroman pattern is evident in the major events in Henry Pelham's life. Born in the country to parents who are all surface charm, young Pelham quickly recognizes their lack of moral and educational depth. He is clever enough to hide his disapproval of their superficiality by assuming a pose of exaggerated indifference. Told he must play his parents' fashionable game of cynical social manipulation to get on in the world, Pelham keeps his doubts about such a policy to himself until he is free from his mother's direct domination. Public school becomes an exercise in opportunism. Pelham's mother explains what gaining knowledge is about: "Remember, my dear, that in all the friends you make at present, you look to the advantage you can derive from them hereafter. That is what we call knowledge of the world; and it is to get the knowledge of the world that you are sent to public school."[13]

At Cambridge Pelham rebels against the expected pattern of undergraduate behavior; he becomes distinguished for not playing the bully, the roué, the fop, or the gamester. But both Eton and Cambridge have been educationally inadequate. While Pelham can make twenty Latin verses in half an hour, construe all the easy Latin authors without an English translation, and read Greek, no one taught him a syllable of English and he knows nothing about English literature or history. "I was," he declares, "in the profoundest ignorance" (6). His round of visits to the best country houses, part of his mother's plan to educate him as a man of the world, only reinforces his boredom at such meaningless social activities. His fashionable continental tour involves him with two women, Mme. d'Anville and the Duchesse de Perpignan. Playing the gallant and flirt, Pelham is forced to fight a duel in Paris for the questionable honor of a woman whom he dislikes and who, he later learns, is indifferent to him.

Returning to England, Pelham canvasses for a seat in Parliament, cynically learning to be all things to all men. He holds no principle dear save that of getting elected for the borough of Buyemall. However, his election places him under the patronage and positive influence of his uncle, Lord Glenmorris, whose Benthamite doctrines Pelham studies. The notion of the greatest good for the greatest number supplants his parents' creed of every man for himself and the devil take us all. Studying James Mill's *On Government,* he comes to accept Glenmorris's beliefs that "the object of education is to instill principles to guide and to instruct the intellect—principles ought to precede facts" (151). Pelham discovers how "inseparably allied is the great science of public policy with that of private morality" (153).

Such studies lead Pelham to reevaluate his character and to revise his earlier affected indifference to thought and feeling. About his first stage of youthful development he says: "My good feelings— for I was not naturally bad—never availed me the least when present temptation came into my way. I had {until Glenmorris's instruction} no guide but passion, no rule but the impulse of the moment. What else could have been the result of my education?" (154). As a result of his studies, Pelham stops looking upon the world "as a game one was to play—fairly, if possible, but where a little cheating was readily allowed." He can "no longer divorce the interests of other men from [his] own; if [he] endeavoured to blind them, it was neither by unlawful means nor for a purely selfish end" (154). But his mother's suspicions about Glenmorris's doctrines lead to Pelham's recall to London.

London becomes Pelham's chief instructor as he applies Glenmorris's theories to real-life situations. Here—in Lord Vincent's political expediency, in Lord Dawton's hypocrisy, and in Lord Guloseton's epicurean sloth—he sees living examples of the separation of public policy from private morality. And, in forays into London low-life, Pelham finds misdirected ambition, ruthlessness, and selfishness in the characters of Jemmy Gordon, Chitterling Crabtree, and Job Jonson. Such scenes of human misery and self-deception only strengthen Pelham's new convictions as experience enables him to translate theory into personal practice. Pelham drops his youthful pose of indifference in order to save Reginald Glanville's reputation. About the indifference he affected earlier he says, "I have always had a great horror of being a hero in scenes, and a still greater antipathy to females in distress as such personal intervention is neither useful nor dignified as common sense never quarrels with anyone" (182). Pelham endangers his own life to discover Tyrrell's murderer. He also comes under the elevating influence of Glanville's sister, Ellen, for whom Pelham undergoes further personal reforms. It is Ellen's love that motivates Pelham's selfless acts on behalf of Glanville.

At the close of the novel Pelham's self-education and passage to maturity are completed. In evaluating his experience, he tells the reader: "If I am less anxious than formerly for a reputation to be acquired in society, I am more eager for honour in the world; and instead of amusing my enemies and the salon, I trust yet to be useful to my friends and to mankind" (477–78). Thus Pelham abandons eccentric exhibitionism and youthful follies for Glenmorris's more edifying Benthamism. He dedicates himself to advancing the general good through benevolent acts of public usefulness rather than pursuing selfish opportunism and ostentatious self-display.

All the subordinate plots in *Pelham* act to reinforce the central bildungsroman action. Parallel to the hero's initiation into manhood are silver-fork, low-life, and political-novel patterns. Much of the power of Pelham's rites of passage is based on Bulwer's highly effective reversal of fashionable novel conventions, which he both satirizes and uses as developmental stages in Pelham's coming of age. Many silver-fork novels routinely exalted high society, uncritically describing the round of events patronized by the social elite—Crockfords and Almacks, rides in Hyde Park, country house weekends, New Market and Goodwood, balls and dinner parties, weddings, continental tours, fashionable watering places, and parliamentary electioneering. But Bulwer satirically turned these ritual set pieces against themselves, showing how hollow and meaningless such events could be. Fashionable life in Bulwer's view is a mechanical world of illusion and sham, pretense and surface appearance, a place where for the sake of the game its participants pretend to be what they are not.

The low-life scenes—a literary genre established by Pierce Egan's novel *Life in London* (1821–24) and its sequel—are used to drive home Bulwer's satire against high society. Low-life gin palaces and gaming "hells" become grotesque, reverse mirror images of fashionable life. And the melodramatic parts of the novel—the secret about Reginald Glanville's mysterious past, Gertrude Douglas's rape and ensuing insanity, the madhouse scenes, Glanville's revenge plot against John Tyrrell, Thomas Thornton's blackmail and murder plots, and Pelham's amateur detective work to clear Glanville of Tyrrell's murder—also support Pelham's apprenticeship story. The antihero, Reginald Glanville, is a passionate, dark, Byronic figure expressly used as a symbolic opposite to Pelham. Glanville represents the reverse of the sophisticated, civilized Pelham; he is ruled by a brooding, inner force of near demonic sensibility. As a figure of strong emotions, Glanville emphasizes the absence of feelings in Pelham's social world. Yet it was not the Byronic dimensions of Bulwer's novel that engaged his readers, but rather Henry Pelham's character, with all his cynical wit and glib worldliness. In *Pelham,* Bulwer finally laid to rest the ghost of Byronism.

The *Disowned* as a Study in Christian Fortitude

Seven months after the publication of *Pelham,* Bulwer rushed another novel into print at the insistence of Henry Colburn his publisher, who wished to capitalize on *Pelham*'s success. Written in less than a year, *The Disowned* was a product of great haste.[14] It was printed anonymously by Colburn in four long volumes amounting to 1,350 pages of text. The reviewer in the *Examiner* was correct when he said that Bulwer "had written *Pelham* for his own pleasure, but *The Disowned* for his publisher."[15] Colburn expressed both his gratitude and his expectation of large sales by giving Bulwer £800 for the copyright. His speculation soon turned to profit, for *The Disowned* was even more successful commercially than *Pelham*. Despite the 1829 date printed on the title page, *The Disowned* was actually published in late 1828—such postdating was fairly common with end-of-the-year books. Bulwer's third published novel was dedicated to his eldest brother, William, in an unsigned dedicatory address. About the book's artistic aims, Bulwer declared in the Advertisement to the 1852 edition that "at the time when the work was written he was engaged in the study of metaphysics and ethics."[16]

The Disowned was Bulwer's first attempt to write what he called a metaphysical novel. To Bulwer a metaphysical novel "was not to be regarded as a mere portraiture of outward society;" indeed "it often wanders from the exact probability of effects in order to bring more strikingly before us the truth of causes." Its main characteristic is the employment of "dim and shadowy allegory which it deserts or resumes at will, making its action but the incarnation of some peculiar and abstract qualities."[17] Bulwer's design for *The Disowned*, according to the preface for the second edition (December 1828), was "not to detail a mere series of events in the history of one individual or another, [but] to Personify certain dispositions influential upon conduct. [For example] Vanity (Talbot); Ambition (Warner); Pride (Lord Borodail); Selfishness and Sensuality (Crauford); Philanthropy (Mordaunt)."[18] In addition, Bulwer claims the gypsy leader King Cole is "the abstract development of love of liberty from the poet's point of view," and John Wolfe represents "the love of liberty under its political aspect." Each character is the allegorical personification of some abstraction. The chief character, Algernon Mordaunt, represents "a type of the Heroism of Christian Philosophy,—a union of love and knowledge placed in the midst of sorrow, and labouring on through the pilgrimage of life, strong in the fortitude that comes from belief in Heaven."[19]

In assigning specific moral qualities to his characters, Bulwer returned to an older narrative tradition, the symbolic or metaphysical romance. Nondramatic in technique, metaphysical romances are not ruled by the canons of realism, which emphasize experience. Rather, the romance is shaped by the power of the author's philosophical vision. To make his didacticism more palatable, Bulwer employed several secondary plots filled with sensational incidents and melo-drama. His son, the poet-novelist Owen Meredith, recognized the perils of writing outside the realistic tradition. He thought that his father failed to see that "the more you raise interest by stirring scenes and a pathetic plot, the greater becomes the impatience at disquisition and digression. Instead of the romance operating as a relief to the philosophy, the philosophy is felt as an encumbrance on the romance."[20]

The design of *The Disowned,* like the design of *Pelham,* is based on a composite of literary conventions—pattern formulas taken from the silver-fork novel, the political reform novel, the Künstlerroman, the urban crime novel, the sensational romance, and the adventure story. Uniting these subordinate patterns is Bulwer's controlling metaphysical thesis concerning the heroic Christian fortitude dis-played by the novel's philosophical hero, Algernon Mordaunt, in the face of adverse fortune and personal tragedy.

Mordaunt represents the novel's moral center, someone against whom the moral success or failure of the other characters is measured. His philosophy is grounded in what Bulwer calls the systematic principle of love, which is a blend of traditional Christian ethics and contemporary Benthamism. Mordaunt believes that the greatest good and the highest personal morality are expressed in disinterested public benevolence, generated by wisdom and achieved through knowledge used for public service in behalf of mankind. Mordaunt's strength of character allows him to triumph over his loss of family name and fortune, over poverty and personal suffering, over the plots and persecutions of Vavasour Mordaunt and Richard Crauford, and over the tragic death of his beloved wife, Isabel, who dies of starvation. Near the end of the novel Mordaunt articulates Bulwer's shaping thesis: "The love of true glory is the most legitimate agent of extensive good. . . . I would say that [personal] ambition is for me no more; not so its effects: but the hope of serving that race whom I have loved as brothers, but who have never known me . . . the hope of serving them is to me, now a far stronger passion than ambition was heretofore; and, whatever for that end the love of fame would have dictated, the love of mankind will teach me still more ardently to perform."[21]

In moral contrast to Mordaunt are Talbot, Richard Crauford, John Wolfe, and Warner. A representation of vanity and self-cen-teredness, Talbot is worldly and ambitious. But his desire to improve

his mind and be a good citizen is selfishly turned inward. Richard
Crauford, based on the real-life forger and swindler Henry Fount-
leroy, represents a reverse side of Mordaunt's philosophy. Crauford
is a wealthy businessman with a reputation for moral piety, but he
is privately driven by lust and grasping self-interest. He hypocrit-
ically mouths all the conventional religious pieties in public, while
in private he is a drunken reprobate and seducer. John Wolfe is a
republican political reformer and visionary idealist who seeks to
achieve the public good through constitutional reform. His idealism
eventually turns to despotism and violence, and he ends by trying
to assassinate Algernon Mordaunt. Like Crauford, Wolfe is executed
at Newgate, his political ambitions ruined by senseless violence.
He failed, Bulwer's narrator argues, because his ambition to improve
the world was motivated not by public service but by selfish egoism.
The painter Warner represents misdirected artistic idealism. Seeking
personal immortality through fame in art, Warner has his hopes
destroyed by Sir Joshua Reynolds's criticism of one of his visionary
historical paintings. Enraged that Reynolds and the public fail to
recognize his merit, Warner commits suicide, refusing to live any
longer in a world that cannot see his artistic greatness. Both Wolfe
and Warner come to grief because their philosophies violate the
common good—both are self-serving instead of selfless.

The Clarence Linden plot—a romantic formula about a disin-
herited youth of genteel birth who eventually restores his name,
title, and fortune—presents problems from the view of architectonic
unity. Linden seems to stand outside Bulwer's allegory, and his
relation to the other characters is superficial at best. It could be
argued that outwardly, at least, he unifies all the other plots, as he
is the only one in the novel whose story intersects those of all the
other characters. He is Mordaunt's friend, Talbot's protége, Warner
and Wolfe's benefactor, and Crauford's acquaintance. But Linden
does not represent any recognizable moral quality, and he does not
undergo any moral growth or dramatize any philosophical position.
At best the Linden story is a part of Bulwer's strategy of using
stirring scenes and pathetic plots to raise reader interest once it bogs
down in passages of philosophical disquisition. Such a strategy,
combined with Bulwer's mannerisms of style and his hasty planning,
makes *The Disowned* a flawed book. Michael Sadleir justly appraised
it as a novel "artificially conceived and carelessly written," one that

could be improved if reduced by one third with its "over-night rhetoric" trimmed by the cool of "next morning's judgment."[22]

Greville: An Unfinished Silver-Fork Satire

Between the publication of *The Disowned* and *Devereux,* Bulwer began work on another *Pelham*-like social satire called *Greville: A Satire upon Fine Life.*[23] But he completed only eight chapters and a sketchy outline for the second and third volumes. This novel remained unfinished for several reasons. Colburn told Bulwer that the public was tired of silver-fork satires like *Pelham* and suggested he try writing a historical novel in the manner of Sir Walter Scott. Bulwer's son thought the real reason "Greville" was never finished was that Bulwer considered the satire both ineffectual and far too personal. As in *Pelham,* Bulwer drew upon real life for *Greville,* and its hero, Clare Greville, was based partly on Frederick Villiers (the model for Henry Pelham) and partly on himself. The fragment manuscript of *Greville* was first printed in his son's biography in 1883.

Today *Greville* is of interest primarily for two reasons: the contrast of its hero to Henry Pelham, and Bulwer's continued interest in assessing Lady Caroline Lamb's character, which is fictionalized in his portrait of Lady Julia Bellenden. Lady Julia is haughty, violent, and exacting, yet capable of "that rare, noble, and devoted love which we dream of between the age of sixteen and twenty-one."[24] Her mind is unquiet and brilliant—half diamonds, half tinsel— and her thoughts are always acting a sort of melodrama. In addition to analyzing Lady Julia Bellenden, Bulwer satirizes the snobbishness of fashionable riders in Hyde Park, the Athenaeum Club, the nude statue of the Duke of Wellington, literary dilettantes at bluestocking salons, and the endemic mindlessness of fashionable social figures who copy each other in a vain attempt to be original. It is clear from Bulwer's two-page outline that, like *Pelham,* "Greville" was to be supported by a melodramatic plot, treating switched identities and past secrets that come to light. Also, Clare Greville and Lady Agnes Percivale were to be united in marriage at the close of the third volume. Whether Greville would overcome his lack of ambition and step forward to claim the distinctions his talents deserve remains uncertain. What is clear is that Colburn's pressure on Bul-

wer to explore the historical or costume-romance genre persuaded
him to leave *Greville* unfinished in order to begin work on *Devereux*.

Devereux and the Vanities of This Life

Devereux was Bulwer's first serious experiment with a historical
subject in fiction. It was published in three volumes on 7 July 1829
by Henry Colburn. Colburn gave Bulwer £1,500 for the copyright,
but the book's sales did not really justify such generous payment.
Devereux was the least popular of Bulwer's early novels while, ironically, it was his favorite. Bulwer dedicated *Devereux* to his friend
at Naples, John Auldjo. In the dedication Bulwer claimed that he
"wished to portray a man flourishing in the last century with the
train of mind and sentiment peculiar to the present; describing a
life, and not its dramatic epitome."[25] Unlike Scott's historical fiction, Bulwer's novel deals "less with the Picturesque than the Real"
(vii). By that Bulwer meant that he was more interested in the
psychology of his historical personages than with the historical forces
actuating their policies. In addition, *Devereux* has some autobiographical significance in the theme of the inheritance and jealousy
among the three brothers in the novel. This theme is loosely based
on Bulwer's own fanciful speculations about who, among his own
brothers, would inherit the family estate at Knebworth.

In the Note to the 1832 edition of *Devereux*, Bulwer avails himself
of the artist's privilege to "place the spectator in the point of view
wherein the light best falls upon the canvas" (vii). He suggests that
to best understand the character of Morton Devereux, his narrator
and hero, the reader should recognize that Devereux was only "dimly
conscious that the tone of his mind harmonized less with his own
age than with that which was to come" (xi). The autobiography
Devereux writes is to be seen as a legacy to the present, and it is
less a romance than the narration of a life. His life, marked by
thwarted ambition, personal sorrow, and some success, leaves him
in a position to do nothing but discover the vanities of this world
and ponder on the hopes of the next as he writes his autobiography.
Devereux's literary reconstruction of his life—the plots to deny him
his rightful inheritance, his adventures in the world to secure his
own livelihood, his personal knowledge of the French and Russian
courts, and his friendship with Bolingbroke—allows him to see that
these experiences are all essential to "the creation of that mixture

of wearied satiety and mournful thought which conducts the Pro-
bationer to the lonely spot in which he is destined to learn at once
the mystery of his past life and to clear his reason from the doubts
that had obscured the future world" (xiii). The significance of this
composite potboiler is not found in its Jesuit-Jacobite conspiracies—
mere stirring and pathetic plot fillers—but in the growth of Morton
Devereux's character, and what he learns about himself as he sorts
and rearranges the incidents of his life into some coherent pattern.
Yet from the standpoint of literary construction *Devereux* is an improvement over *The Disowned,* if still some distance from the in-
genuity found in Bulwer's later historical romances.

There is no doubt that Bulwer took pains to research his material
accurately. But the parade of documentation in his footnotes gives
the novel an air of pedantry instead of verisimilitude. Only in his
treatment of Bolingbroke does history briefly come alive. Michael
Sadleir is correct in noting that Bulwer's personal interest in Bolingbroke arose from his sympathy for the "defeat of this lofty,
aspiring but essentially aristocratic mind at the hands of lesser and
more commonplace men than himself. . . ."[26] Such a theme appealed to Bulwer's romantic love of nobility in degradation. However, Bulwer's portrait of Bolingbroke earned him condemnation
from the Millites at the *Westminster Review* who, in a critique of
Devereux in October, 1829, expressed their dislike for the novel. It
may be that Bulwer's movement away from Saint-Simonism and
Benthamism to Tory democracy (Disraelism) can be traced to his
study of Bolingbroke's *Patriot King,* which was an important tract
in Tory democratic theory. In the last analysis *Devereux* is the weakest
of all Bulwer's historical and costume-romances, a verdict supported
by the book's lack of popularity with contemporary readers and
modern critics.

Chapter Three
Crime and Newgate Novels

In both *Pelham* and *The Disowned* Bulwer included episodes of crime and mystery as stirring plot fillers, secondary in artistic importance to the domestic themes organizing each novel. However in *Paul Clifford* (1830), his next novel, he changed aesthetic priorities. This shift originated in his desire to reform the penal code, which led him to quit the "loftier regions of imagination" to examine the way English society treated criminals.[1] The result was a sensational thriller almost wholly centered on crime and mystery, a daring propaganda novel that boldly attacked the criminal laws for the brutal frequency of capital punishment.

Paul Clifford was Bulwer's fifth novel, written when he was twenty-eight and published in three volumes on 30 April 1830 by Colburn and Bentley. It became an immediate commercial success. The first edition, the largest printing of any modern novel up to that time, sold all its copies the first day.[2] To boost sales, Colburn and Bentley skillfully puffed the novel with advance publicity. They slyly hinted to the public that many of the novel's characters were burlesque portraits, done "in the utmost good humour," of the king and leading politicians of the day.[3] In the dedicatory letter, Bulwer acknowledged one of the original sources for *Paul Clifford*—William Godwin's suggestion that he adapt the idea behind John Gay's *The Beggar's Opera* (1728). Other identifiable sources were William Jerdan, editor of the *Literary Gazette,* who expressed interest in having Bulwer write a political satire; William Godwin's *An Enquiry Concerning Political Justice* (1793); Jeremy Bentham's *Indications Respecting Lord Eldon; The Newgate Calendar;* and Elizabeth Inchbauld's novel *Nature and Art* (1796).

Paul Clifford was the first important Newgate novel published, and the first of Bulwer's four crime novels, followed by *Eugene Aram* (1832), *Night and Morning* (1841), and *Lucretia* (1846). Novels like *Paul Clifford* belong to a class of fiction in which the hero is a criminal. This feature separates Newgate fiction from other crime novels such as gothic novels, picaresque and rogue stories, or romantic accounts of banditry—pirate, poacher, smuggler, or gypsy stories. In these, the criminal is depicted as a villain or a secondary character.

Many Newgate novels are based upon the careers of actual criminals whose exploits figure in *The Newgate Calendar*—a semiofficial account of criminal cases, trials, confessions, and executions. The hero can be a highwayman (the aristocrat of crime), a middle-class stock swindler, a common housebreaker, or a humble servant who robs or kills his employer. While Newgate novels exhibit great variation in subject and treatment, Keith Hollingsworth has identified three thematic variants among them. The criminal may be: 1) the object of a search in an exciting chase-adventure romance; 2) a representative victim of social evils in a problem novel calling for legal or social reforms; or 3) the subject of a moral or psychological case study in a story examining criminal motivation.[4] About fourteen Newgate novels appeared between 1830 and 1846; several, like William Harrison Ainsworth's *Rookwood* (1834) and *Jack Sheppard* (1839), were modeled directly on Bulwer's *Paul Clifford*.[5]

Contemporary periodical reviewers tended to lump Newgate novels together as if they constituted a recognizable school of fiction. But they did not coalesce into a school because they shared few internal qualities that could unify them. Studied individually, they feature such diversity that it is impossible to identify any common pattern of construction or to find any similarity of artistic intent among them. Whatever unity they had originated solely from critical opposition to them on moral, aesthetic, or political grounds. A reviewer wishing to condemn a book had only to place it into the odious Newgate category. Such critical opposition led to a public controversy fought out in the pages of the influential magazines of the day. A central issue in this controversy became the degree of moral responsibility an author owed to his readers and to society. The ubiquitous Victorian Young Person was invoked by moralists to remind Newgate sensationalists that conventional moral sensibilities must not be shocked. Critics charged Newgate novelists with making vice and crime appear attractive by glamorous and sensationalized treatment of the criminal. Bulwer especially bore the critical stigma of showing unbecoming authorial sympathy for the criminal in his Newgate novels. Practically all Newgate writers were censured for familiarizing their readers with scenes of crime and vice to a degree thought socially dangerous. Many conservative

critics believed that placing such unwholesome fiction in the hands
of the urban working classes endangered the social order. In particular they claimed that Newgate fiction increased crime and social
disorder by depicting the governing class in unflattering and irrev-
erent terms.[6]

Paul Clifford and Society as Open War

Representing the ruling class as highwaymen plundering the British public—even if done with lighthearted humor—certainly bor-
ders on irreverence to authority. But such a political allegory is at
the heart of *Paul Clifford*. Bulwer's novel contains three main thematic divisions: it is a propaganda novel attacking the penal code
and those who administer it; a roman à clef political burlesque, part
satire and part allegory, that suggests that politicians are no better
than thieves; and a literary satire against journalist Dr. William
Maginn and two contemporary magazines. In addition *Paul Clifford*
has a traditional romantic plot about an abducted child, a mysterious
dual identity, a judge who sentences his own son to hang, and a
family's secrets coming to light. Uniting all these compositional
strands is a serious thesis that the law is an instrument of class
control used by the ruling class to enrich itself and to set the various
classes in society at war with each other. In this view of an openly
warring society, Bulwer's novel parallels William Godwin's argument in *An Enquiry Concerning Political Justice* (1793). Godwin as-
serts: "The superiority of the rich, being thus unmercifully exercised,
must inevitably expose them to reprisals; and the poor man will be
induced to regard the state of society as a state of war, an unjust
combination, not for protecting every man in his rights and securing
to him the means of existence, but for engrossing all its advantages
to a few favored individuals and reserving for the portion of the rest
want, dependence and misery."[7]

One victim of this social war is young Paul Clifford, whose moral
corruption by the forces of society and subsequent career as a highwayman illustrate the ideas organizing the problem-novel section.
The context for judging Paul and society is articulated in the closing
lines of the 1848 preface. There Bulwer argues that environment
and circumstance combine to create the criminal. If we wish to
redeem the victim, he says, we must mend the circumstance. In
Paul's story Bulwer calls attention to all the social forces that cause

his hero to turn to crime. Orphaned at an early age, Paul is raised by a drunken foster mother, Margery (Peg) Lobkins and her pickpocket friend, Dummie Dunnaker. His earliest years are spent at the Mug, a gin "hell" kept by mother Lobkins and used as a meeting place by a number of London criminals. The dashing, splendidly attired highwaymen who spend their money at the Mug fascinate Paul. Impressed by their pretensions to gentility, their cynical underworld humor, and their ready cash, he falls under the influence of the foppish highwayman Augustus Tomlinson. Such bad social influences soon lead Paul into trouble. Like the title character in Dickens's *Oliver Twist,* Paul is falsely arrested and charged as a pickpocket. Found guilty, he is sentenced to three months at Bridewell in the house of correction.

Bulwer's narrator argues that Paul is a victim of circumstance:

Hitherto thou has seen Paul honest in the teeth of circumstances. Despite the contagion of the Mug, despite his associates in Fish Lane, despite his intimacy with Long Ned, thou has seen him brave temptation, and look forward to some other career than that of robbery or fraud. [Here the narrator reviews all Paul's struggles to remain honest.] . . . His present circumstances, it may hereafter be seen, made the cause of a great change in his desires; and the conversation he held that night with . . . Augustus [Tomlinson] went more towards fitting him for the hero of this work than all the habits of his childhood or the scenes of his earlier youth.[8]

Escaping from Bridewell with Tomlinson, Paul joins his companion in robbing a farmer to secure food and clothing. This robbery is Paul's first criminal act; he is convinced that he can no longer return to a life of respectability. At sixteen he declares war on society. A year later he assumes the alias of Captain Lovett and leads his own band of highwaymen. For seven years Paul earns a notorious underworld reputation as a "knight of the crossroads." While he works the roads outside London, he establishes a separate, genteel life as a fashionable man of the town, calling himself Captain Clifford. Paul's dual existence—highwayman and West End society man—enables Bulwer to show that there is little difference between vulgar and fashionable vice. At Bath Paul falls in love with Lucy Brandon, the daughter of a well-meaning but empty-headed country squire. As his love for her is genuine, he plans to quit crime and return to an honest life. But before he can do so, he and his gang are captured in a robbery and tried before Judge William Brandon, Lucy's uncle.

Paul's closing speech at his trial summarizes Bulwer's indictment of the law. In it are heard the echoes of the social doctrines of William Godwin and Jean-Jacques Rousseau. Paul declares to Judge Brandon:

Your laws are but of two classes; the one makes criminals, the other punishes them. I have suffered by the one;—I am about to perish by the other. . . . Seven years ago I was sent to the house of correction for an offence which I did not commit. I went thither, a boy who had never infringed a single law; I came forth, in a few weeks, a man who was prepared to break all laws! . . . Your legislation made me what I am! and it now destroys me, as it has destroyed thousands, for being what it made me! . . . Let those whom the law protects consider it a protection: when did it ever protect me? When did it ever protect the poor man? The government of a state, the institutions of law, profess to provide for all those who 'obey'. Mark! a man hungers—do you feed him? He is naked— do you clothe him? If not, you break your covenant, you drive him back to the first law of nature, and you hang him, not because he is guilty, but because you left him naked and starving! (35:439–41).

As Brandon begins to pronounce sentence on Paul, word reaches him that Paul is his own son. Stunned by the news, Brandon still pronounces sentence—death by hanging. But through influence, Brandon gets Paul's sentence commuted to transportation to Australia for life. Sometime later Paul escapes from Australia and joins Lucy Brandon in America; there they marry and Paul becomes an honest and productive citizen. Bulwer ends the novel with a quotation from John Wilkes arguing that "the very worst use to which you can put a man is to hang him!" (36:466).

Part of the book's power comes from being a roman à clef— actual persons appear under the guise of fiction. Readers in 1830 were particularly interested in Bulwer's depiction of well-known politicians of both parties as highwaymen. The key to the real identities of these characters was provided by Bulwer's wife, Rosina, in a letter to her friend Mary Greene on 26 May 1830. According to Rosina the members of the good company of thieves were Gentleman George (King George IV), Fighting Attie (the Duke of Wellington), Old Bags (Lord Eldon), Long Ned Pepper (Lord Ellenborough), Scarlet Jem (Sir James Scarlet), Bachelor Bill (the

Duke of Devonshire), Harry Finish (Lord Henry de Ros), the Sallow Gentleman (William Huskisson), Allfair (Lord Alvanley), Augustus Tomlinson (The Whig Party), Peter McGrawler (The Scottish Nation), and Mobbing Francis (Sir Frances Burdett).[9] All the other characters in *Paul Clifford* are imaginary. Bulwer's political satire is directed against those politicians who belonged to the reactionary wings of both political parties—hidebound old Tories, Canningite new Tories tainted by mercantile politics, and reactionary Whigs. In Bulwer's view they were men "who accepted none of the duties of their rank" and lacked all desire to solve any of the serious social and political problems of the day.[10] As politicians, they were guided by the maxim that when in difficult political waters, the best course was no course at all. By drawing a symbolic connection between highwaymen, politicians, and the law, Bulwer suggests that there is little difference in effect among the law, the government, and organized thievery.

A literary satire controls the last component of Bulwer's novel; it is aimed at journalist William Maginn and the *Athenaeum* and *Fraser's* magazines. In Rosina Bulwer's key, the pothouse scribe Peter MacGrawler was identified as the Scottish nation, an idea that Keith Hollingsworth has contradicted.[11] MacGrawler, Hollingsworth claims, is actually Irish journalist Dr. William Maginn, the editor of *Fraser's Magazine*. In *Paul Clifford* MacGrawler is editor of an obscure periodical called the *Asinaeum,* whose editorial policy is that whatever is popular is always bad. Under MacGrawler's tutelage, Paul learns the three branches of literary criticism—"to tickle, to slash, and to plaster" (5:45). The parallel between MacGrawler's fall in fortunes—from magazine editor to a cook for the highwaymen—and Maginn's ruined political fortunes and dismissal from a journal because of irresponsibility was an insult that must have been apparent to many contemporary journalists. Maginn recognized it and lashed out at Bulwer in his review of *Paul Clifford* in *Fraser's.* He claimed that "the author [Bulwer] has done this to take his revenge of *Blackwood's Magazine* and of ourselves, because we have honestly expressed our several opinions—that Mr. Lytton Bulwer is no novelist."[12]

Paul Clifford is a lighthearted book despite its radical political thesis; it is a novel written by a young author who takes up his subject with gusto and enjoyment. Bulwer's grandson believed that "those who read *Paul Clifford* in search of a good story will find one."[13] This seemed to be the general opinion of those who read it when it was first published, though many were shocked by a novel with a highwayman hero. Some readers resented the virtues ascribed to Paul and the vices attributed to William Brandon, the lawyer. But there is no doubt that the novel's good humor carried it a long way with the reviewers who ignored the moral question of a novel with a criminal as hero. Also forgotten was the book's radical thesis about society at war with itself. Most reviewers enjoyed the fun of identifying politicians as thieves. *Paul Clifford,* on the whole, received favorable reviews. The *Examiner* thought "the satire is ever in the right direction,"[14] the *Spectator* termed it an "exceedingly clever work,"[15] and the *Monthly Review* praised the trial scene but felt that the criminal slang was not proper for the eyes of females.[16] William Godwin and the Corn-Law poet Ebenezer Elliott both wrote Bulwer letters of praise about *Paul Clifford.* In his letter of 13 May 1830, Godwin said, "There are parts of the book that I read with transport. There are many parts of it so divinely written that my first impulse was to throw my implements of writing into the fire."[17]

Eugene Aram as the Mark of Cain Idealized

The popular success of *Paul Clifford* brought Bulwer to the public's notice as a rising literary star; he was rightly seen in 1830 as the preeminent leader of the younger generation of novelists. To capitalize on his popularity, he wrote another crime novel, *Eugene Aram,* which Colburn and Bentley brought out in three volumes in January 1832. It was reprinted in one volume in November 1833 as number thirty-four in Bentley's popular standard novel series priced at six shillings. As the second of Bulwer's Newgate novels, it too has crime for its subject; but unlike *Paul Clifford,* it attacks no social evils and prescribes no political reforms. Its leading character is a murderer. Bulwer based his novel on an actual criminal case, that of the 1744 murder of Daniel Clarke by Eugene Aram and Richard Houseman.

Ironically, the historical Aram touched Bulwer in a personal way. In 1829 Bulwer learned that Aram had been engaged occasionally by his grandfather to tutor his daughters at Heydon Hall, Judge Bulwer's home. This discovery led Bulwer to collect local information about Aram. During his research, he met Admiral Burney, who once studied at King's Lynn, where Aram served as an usher.[18]

From Burney, Bulwer received details about Aram's connection with the Lester family, material he used almost verbatim in the novel. Another source for the novel was a sensational murder, quite similar to the Aram case, committed in Spain during the late 1820s. It involved a scholarly Spanish priest who robbed and murdered a man to finance his book purchases. The Spanish case sparked a revival of interest in Aram.[19] Such interest was furthered by the 1829 publication of Thomas Hood's poem, *The Dream of Eugene Aram,* in his annual, the *Gem.* Bulwer read Hood's poem and became fascinated with the theme of a conscience branded with the mark of Cain, a theme he first used in a narrative sketch, "Monos and Daimonos," reprinted in *The Student* (1835).

Bulwer prepared a dramatic sketch about Aram at the same time he wrote the novel. The play, a fragment containing less than two acts, was later printed in all editions of *Eugene Aram,* beginning with the 1833 Bentley edition. It is of interest because of Bulwer's treatment of Aram's motivation for murdering Clarke. In the play the crime is represented as the premeditated act of a cold-blooded criminal. This contrasts with the novel, where Aram is drawn as a quiet, thoughtful, and gentle scholar, goaded by illness, poverty, hunger, and overwork of the mind into a single, terrible act of violence at variance with his whole nature. When the play was published in the *New Monthly Magazine* prior to the novel's publication, Ebenezer Elliott wrote Bulwer suggesting he idealize Aram to create more reader sympathy. Elliott's advice may have led Bulwer to recast Aram's motivation for the novel.[20]

In the preface to the first edition of *Eugene Aram* (1831), Bulwer declared that his artistic intention was to "impart to this Romance something of the nature of Tragedy."[21] In the preface to the 1840 edition, he argued that the novel is best understood as a case study of criminal motivation; it examines the physical circumstances compelling Aram to crime, and its power stems from observing the moral consequences of his guilty act. To Bulwer the examination of such a subject must cause the thoughtful reader to recognize "great and . . . moral truths" that "force themselves on the notice and sink deep into the heart" (xiii). Stories like *Eugene Aram,* Bulwer claimed in the preface to the 1849 edition, "belong to that legitimate class of fiction which illustrates life and truth, and only deals with crime as the recognized agency of pity and terror in the conduct of tragic narrative" (xv). Bulwer also made important textual changes for the 1849 edition. In the preface he said he was convinced that the historical Eugene Aram was innocent of both the premeditated design and the deed of murder. As a consequence, he altered the novel, rewriting Aram's closing narrative and acquitting him of any participation in Daniel Clarke's murder. All editions of the novel published after 1849 depict Aram as guiltless in the murder.

The central action of *Eugene Aram* treats the temptation, fall, and guilty remorse of the book's flawed, tragic, thirty-five-year-old scholar, Eugene Aram. At its core the novel is a psychological case study of criminal motivation. The fall of Bulwer's high-minded hero stems from Aram's intellectual pride, his thirst for arcane truth, his superstitious belief in fate, and his struggles against poverty and hunger. But the most important cause driving Aram to crime is his entanglement in the web of his own false reasoning. In order to continue his research and purchase needed equipment, he resorts to robbery, and through twisted Benthamite reasoning, he convinces himself that a single crime committed to advance the general good of mankind is not really a crime at all. His guilt and suffering work to advance Bulwer's controlling moral thesis, which argues that the foundation of all virtue is fortitude in the face of adversity. In addition, the novel's composite design reflects Bulwer's success in taking gothic and romantic literary themes—the Faust, Byronic, Manfred, wandering Jew, and Cain associations with Aram—and blending them with Newgate crime realism, producing what he called in the text a romance of real life.[22] In secondary design, *Eugene Aram* is both a metaphysical quest story and a detective thriller.

Eugene Aram achieved immediate popularity with contemporary readers, but reviewers were divided about the novel. Some, like the reviewer in the *Athenaeum,* found in it manifest genius. The *Spectator* approved of the novel, seeing nothing wrong with the idealized portrait Bulwer drew of Aram.[23] To the critic at the *Monthly Review, Eugene Aram* was Bulwer's best book yet; he saw in it "a fine tone of Christian philosophy."[24] *Fraser's,* however, led the attack against *Eugene Aram,* labeling it another Newgate Calendar production by an author whose sensibility uniquely qualified him to write such literature. William Maginn, still smarting from the satire against him in *Paul Clifford,* charged Bulwer with "awakening sympathy with interesting criminals, and wasting sensibilities on the scaffold and the goal."[25]

Later in the literary season, Maginn and John Gibson Lockhart got up a satirical parody of *Eugene Aram* called "Elizabeth Brownrigge: A Tale," which ran anonymously in *Fraser's Magazine* from 6 August to 6 September 1832. It was written, its authors slyly claimed in their dedication letter, by writers eager to find success by copying the works of Bulwer. The tale closely imitates *Eugene Aram* at numerous points and mocks Bulwer's stylistic mannerisms, emotional rhetoric, and inflated prose.[26]

One tribute to Bulwer, however, came from Regency-era sportswriter and novelist Pierce Egan, the elder, author of the popular Tom and Jerry series, *Life in London* (1821–24). Convinced that the mantle of chronicler of London low-life now belonged to Bulwer, Egan presented him with the caul of executed murderer John Thurtell. History does not record Bulwer's response to this unique treasure.[27] Yet in Egan's tribute lies a significant fact: as a result of his six published novels to date, Bulwer was clearly recognized as the most popular novelist of his time. Though vilified by Maginn and the *Fraser's* circle, Bulwer wrote novels containing ideas and actions that aroused great public interest.

Night and Morning and the Social Distinctions between Vice and Crime

Nine years passed before Bulwer employed crime again as a subject for a novel. In the interim he used other subjects and wrote in other genres, namely, metaphysical and historical fiction, historical drama, and nonfiction history. His third crime romance, *Night and Morning,* was printed by Saunders and Otley in January 1841 in three volumes. The novel was dedicated to Charles Tennyson D'Eyncourt, M.P., at whose house, Bayens Manor, Bulwer had written parts of the novel.

According to the preface for the 1843 edition, Bulwer had three artistic aims in the novel. First, he sought to deal fearlessly with the distinctions society makes between vice and crime, between "the corrupting habits and the violent act."[28] Second, he wished "to lift the mask from the timid selfishness which too often . . . bears the name of 'Respectability' " (xi). And third, he suggested that books alone do not make people conscious of their true moral strength. Bulwer wished to reaffirm that "Life is the great Schoolmaster, Experience the mighty Volume" (xii). We may achieve much real knowledge, Bulwer claims, if we cling fast to two simple maxims: be "honest in temptation, and in Adversity believe in God" (xii). These maxims shape *Night and Morning* and are dramatized in his hero, Philip Beaufort, and heroine, Fanny, who in their "primitive and natural characters—with aid more from life than books; from courage the one, from affection the other—[are] examples of resolute Manhood and tender Womanhood" (xii).

Night and Morning was a bold fictional experiment on Bulwer's part. In it he employs crime and melodrama to unfold a metaphysical vision of life where "truth and falsehood dwell undisturbed and unseparated" (viii). Bulwer seeks to convert his readers from materialistic values and to place them on the right road to spiritual salvation. Such a change of heart is to be achieved by the power of Bulwer's moral vision, which stems from his presentation of two contending worlds: the actual (the material) and the ideal (the spiritual). To Bulwer the actual world is a product of soulless material progress, a place where vice, crime, and selfishness coexist, sometimes behind the mask of respectability. To survive the strife of such a world below requires a healthful confidence in the world above. And to retain this spiritual confidence presupposes a commitment to an ideal world of the mind where honesty against temptation and faith in adversity are reinforced by love, courage, kindness, and generosity.

The central action in *Night and Morning* follows young Philip Beauford's struggles to survive in a materialistic world that places great importance on birth, money, and family connection. Over the ensuing years, Philip tries to earn his livelihood honestly, to support his brother Sidney, to reestablish his name, and to recover legal possession of Fernside—and in time he succeeds in all these efforts. Yet for Bulwer the significance of the novel lies not in Philip's return to material well-being, but in the formation of his moral character, which is threatened by his poverty, his injudicious companions (George Smith and William Gawtrey), and his initial bitterness against his uncle's selfish exploitation of his misfortune. Unlike Sidney, whose adoption returns him to financial security and gives him a formal education, Philip gains moral growth from hard practical experience. In this sense Philip dramatizes Bulwer's thesis stated in the preface, that life is the great schoolmaster and experience is its mighty volume. He overcomes the disadvantages of poverty, withstands the temptations to live outside the law, and in time replaces his hatred of his uncle with a reliance on God's providence.

As Bulwer's hero, Philip exemplifies the virtues of courage and faith. His character evolves from that of a strong-willed, proud, and violently impetuous boy nearly consumed by fiery thoughts of revenge to that of a mature man who is thoughtful, temperate, and refined in moral sensibility. Though he is "so little lettered, Life has taught him a certain poetry of sentiment and idea" (4.5.355). He develops a "largeness of idea and a nobility of impulse" which leads him to recognize two advantages from his youthful days of error: "First, the humiliation it brought, curbed in some measure a pride that might otherwise have been arrogant and unamiable; and second . . . his profound gratitude to Heaven for his deliverance from the snares that had beset his youth gave his future the guide of an earnest and heartfelt faith. . . . He never despaired; for nothing now could shake his belief in one directing Providence" (4.5.356). Such moral growth stems from an epiphany-like warning Philip experiences at the moment he is tempted to join William Gawtrey's gang of coiners. While walking the streets of Paris, he sees three carved figures adorning a bridge; these are emblems signifying time, energy, and faith. Philip is saved from his own worst self by recognizing that these virtues are the key to his moral salvation. From that moment, he vows to shape his life around them. Time, energy, and faith are also concepts central to Bulwer's moral vision; they are the virtues needed for salvation in a sickly civilization dominated by materialism.

To contemporary readers the rogue, crime, and detective sections of *Night and Morning* were far more exciting than Bulwer's metaphysical homilies. Yet the crime scenes reinforce the novel's didacticism because they provide Philip with the occasion for his temptation, self-evaluation, and reformation. In addition, they give Bulwer the opportunity to dramatize part of his dual thesis about society's unfair distinctions between crime and vice. Specifically, Bulwer examines the differences between the harsh and immediate penalties exacted from those who break the law, and the general indifference of respectable society to those who may devote an entire lifetime to private vice, escaping both the law and public censure. Bulwer does not expect the law to reach vice, as it does crime, but he hopes that his novel will so strike off the differences between them as to forcefully appeal to his readers' consciences.

Critical reception of *Night and Morning* was mixed. The *Athenaeum* thought Bulwer's novel was strained in its effect. It was "not so much a work of art, as a work of artifice."[29] On this point the reviewer in *Tait's Magazine* agreed; he believed the novel was good, but "exaggerated and overstrained in energy."[30] In addition the *Tait's* reviewer judged Bulwer's depiction of William Gawtrey "original and powerful" but feared that moralistic critics would take exception to him.[31]

John Forster raised the same point in a long and generally favorable review in the *Examiner*. He complained that Philip Beaufort, the novel's hero, never fully recovers his moral position after his association with Gawtrey because in Gawtrey "the limits between good and evil are scarcely marked throughout with sufficient clearness and precision." Such moral ambiguity, Forster argued, creates the "danger of suggesting a false sympathy with crime."[32] Modern readers will find little substance in Forster's objections to Gawtrey, but in 1841 the unwritten rules governing how evil characters could be depicted in fiction were rigid and not easily broached. No novelist, as Forster reminded Bulwer, ought to ascribe an atrocious action to a generous principle. If *Night and Morning* achieved nothing else, it extended the boundaries allowed the Victorian novelist in selecting his subject matter.

Lucretia and the Influence of Home Education on Later Conduct

Bulwer's crime novel, *Lucretia; or, The Children of Night,* was published in December 1846 in three volumes by Saunders and Otley. Bulwer's grandson wrote in 1948 that it was his grandfather's worst book by far, as it dealt with "the vilest, cruellest, most despicable human beings—criminals without a single redeeming feature."[33] *Lucretia* proved a troublesome book for Bulwer, raising an immediate storm of protest from reviewers on moral grounds. The critics, Bulwer complained, never understood the book's real moral argument; they seemed content to misjudge it as a melodramatic romance of homicide. Written at the same time as *The Caxtons* (1848–49), his vastly popular domestic novel, *Lucretia* shared with it the same purpose, namely, to "show the influence of home education, of early circumstance and example, upon after character and conduct."[34] While *The Caxtons* seeks "the comic elements of

humour and agreeable emotion," *Lucretia,* its complementary opposite in mood, focuses on the "darker side of human nature,"
necessarily resorting "to the tragic elements of awe and distress" (v).

In the preface to the first edition, Bulwer identified another
objective. He wished to examine impatience, which was the principle vice of the day and was caused by the hot pursuit of success
and the desire for instant wealth. This nearly national mania "to
press forward," to "thirst after quick returns to ingenious toil," and
to search for "short cuts to the goal" were some of "the diseased
symptoms of the times"—signs in Bulwer's view almost synonymous with the "cant phrase, the March of Intellect" (vii–viii).
Consequently, *Lucretia* is designed to illustrate that labor and patience "are the true schoolmasters on earth" (viii). The novel's moral
is that "toil in pursuit of knowledge is the best knowledge we can
attain . . . that it is not wealth suddenly acquired which is de-
serving of homage, but the virtues which a man exercises in the
slow pursuit of wealth,—the abilities so called forth, the self-denials
so imposed" (viii).

Like *Eugene Aram* before it, *Lucretia* was based on an actual criminal
case, on the forgeries and murders committed by Thomas Griffiths
Wainewright (1794–1847) and his wife, Frances. Bulwer appeared
to deny this in his 1846 preface to *Lucretia* by claiming that he
compiled his novel from two separate criminal cases. He contended
that neither of the actual criminals, unlike the two in his novel,
were known to each other in real life. But this was mere subterfuge
to protect himself from a possible libel suit by Mrs. Wainewright,
who was still living in England in 1846. Years later in his biography
Bulwer's grandson confirmed that Wainewright and his wife were
the originals for the fictitious Gabriel Varney and Lucretia
Clavering.[35]

Lucretia is a composite novel: a political novel describing the year
before the passage of the first Reform Bill of 1832; an anti–French
Revolution novel; and a sensational crime thriller featuring changelings, switched identities, and melodramatic coincidences. At its
center is a shaping thesis about how intellect without ethical guidance leads to evil. The central plot features an amoral villainess of
commanding intellect who, driven by jealous revenge, attempts to
poison her rivals to secure a large fortune.

In its focus on an evil woman of ambitious intellect, *Lucretia* closely parallels Mrs. Frances Trollope's earlier thriller *Tremordyn Cliff* (1835), in which her lead character, Lady Augusta Delaporte, exhibits nearly the same early education, malevolent intellect, and lust of revenge and power. In Mrs. Trollope's romance, the heroine concentrates all her awesome intellectual gifts on supplanting her brother as heir to the family fortune. Similar in theme, *Lucretia* was to become the source for several mid-Victorian sensation novels about female characters who kill for money and property—specifically, Mary Elizabeth Braddon's Lucy Audley of *Lady Audley's Secret* (1862) and Wilkie Collins's Lydia Gwilt of *Armadale* (1864–66).

Bulwer's novel is divided into two parts. The first, set in revolutionary France during the 1790s and in England in 1801, traces the formative influences on Lucretia Clavering's character. It illustrates Bulwer's ruling thesis that home education, early circumstance, and example determine character and conduct. The second part begins twenty-seven years later on 8 September 1831, the day of William IV's coronation. It traces the results of Lucretia Clavering's early education on her character.

Central is Gabriel Varney and Lucretia's plot to poison the two remaining heirs, Percival St. John (Vernon's son) and Helen Mainwaring (William and Susan's daughter). But a servant, a former London crossing sweeper named Beck, witnesses Lucretia's attempts to poison Helen and exposes her to Percival. In revenge, Lucretia stabs Beck with the poisoned spring of her Borgia ring and too late discovers that he is her long-missing son by a previous marriage. Lucretia shows the first signs of insanity when Beck falls dead at her feet, blood gushing from his mouth and splattering her dress. Placed in a private asylum, Lucretia becomes a "grisly, squalid, ferocious mockery of a human being, more appalling and more fallen than Dante ever fabled in his spectres" (epilogue, 446). Varney escapes to London, where he is arrested by Bow Street runners for embezzlement. He is tried, found guilty, and transported for life to New South Wales, where he becomes a Caliban among Calibans, falling to the lowest level of convict society. Bulwer closes the novel arguing that in *Lucretia* he sought to teach by example. Olivier Dalibard represents the fate of the man "who only cultivates the reason," Varney exemplifies the youth "who develops but the animal as he stifles the man," and Lucretia Dalibard symbolizes unrestrained

ego and ambition, which end "in the laugh of the maniac murderess" (epilogue, 449–50).

From early December 1846, the reviews of *Lucretia* were negative,
if not openly hostile. The *Athenaeum* panned it, calling *Lucretia* a
"bad book of a bad school." Its reviewer especially objected to
Bulwer's overuse of melodramatic coincidence, warning him that
the novel's improbabilities and patchwork construction constituted
a serious artistic flaw. Bulwer, he continued, should "consult the
permanence of his reputation—which is perilled by the present
work."[36] The *Spectator's* notice condemned the book for exhibiting
a marked "moral unhealthiness of mind."[37] But the most damaging
attack came in the *Times,* where Bulwer was severely taken to task
for tampering with the trustful minds of his readers. At the close
of the *Times's* notice, the anonymous reviewer warned Bulwer that
if he wished to be useful to his generation as a writer, he should
"avoid for the future all novels 'founded upon fact.' "[38] The *Morning
Herald* complained that Bulwer was at the head of those writers who
depraved the public mind; *Lucretia* was "as mischievious as those
other works of the same author."[39] The *Herald* reviewer concluded
by asserting that as a result of Newgate novels, "the great body of
people are too apt to sympathize with criminals."[40]

Bulwer became frightened by the increasing chorus of public
attacks on him; he was especially worried by the *Times's* review
because of the paper's great influence and wide circulation. He
wrongly believed that his old enemy, William Makepeace Thackeray, wrote the *Times* article, as it resembled in tone and style
Thackeray's earlier attacks against him in *Fraser's* and *Punch.*

Bulwer suspected that an organized cabal had been put together
against him, and he worried about how best to combat it. He
contemplated three ways to defend himself. The first and the silliest
was to call Thackeray out and fight him in a duel. But cooler heads
prevailed. Thanks to the advice of John Forster and Albany Fonblanque, this absurd scheme never matured.[41] Bulwer's second response took the form of a pamphlet published on 23 January 1847,
called *A Word to the Public.* In it he defended his novels, claiming
that crime had a legitimate and useful place in literature. Great
crime, Bulwer insisted, "is the highest province of fiction—it has
always been so considered—from the Greeks to Shakespeare. It is
the analysis of the prodigies thus startling that is the true work of
the Master."[42] His third option was to cease writing Newgate novels

altogether. This he did after 1846, never again producing a novel solely about crime with a criminal as the hero.

Fears that his publisher, Saunders and Otley, would abandon him if he were subjected to further public condemnation finally decided Bulwer in this course. In the end his claim that crime was the highest province of fiction and his demand that an author should be free to pursue his own subjects were silenced by the prudish objections of Mrs. Grundy speaking on behalf of the Victorian Young Person. Bulwer left Newgate crime fiction to G. W. M. Reynolds and the Salisbury Square writers of working-class penny dreadfuls, who continued to produce these thrillers during the late 1840s and early 1850s. But in the 1860s crime fiction would again become fashionable among middle-class readers, reappearing this time as the mid-Victorian sensation novel.

Chapter Four
Bildungsromane and Metaphysical Novels

The publication of *Paul Clifford* in 1830 marked the end of Bulwer's second stage of artistic development, his realistic phase, featuring novels shaped by the social doctrines of Jeremy Bentham and William Godwin. These novels—his Utilitarian silver-fork satires, Godwinian crime thrillers, and problem novels (tendenzromane)—addressed public concerns and debated political issues, thus reversing the direction of his earlier Byronic novels with their romantic and intensely private vision.

Yet ever the romantic idealist, Bulwer grew restless working in the realistic mode. Evidence of this is found in the preface to the 1845 edition of *Paul Clifford,* where he claimed that the novel closed an era in his self-education as a writer. From *Pelham* to *Paul Clifford* he had "rather observe[d] than imagine[d]—rather deal[t] with the ordinary surface of human life," but after *Eugene Aram,* he saw "the first gleams from a fairer fancy" that rested on "more ideal images."[1] Feeling that realism restricted his imaginative powers, he returned to the romance, and as a consequence the novels written after *Eugene Aram* form a third phase in the corpus of his writings, his metaphysical novels.

Bulwer's disenchantment with the realistic mode stemmed only partly from his inherently romantic temperament. It also arose from his preference for the Italian ideal school of art over the low Dutch realists, his increasing hostility to materialism, positivism, and empiricism, and his recent acquaintanceship with German philosophic idealism—in particular, his interest in Schiller's distinctions between epic and dramatic poetry adapted to the novel. Schiller's influence is seen in an essay Bulwer wrote that appeared as the preface to the 1835 edition of *The Disowned.* In this important essay, entitled "On the Different Kinds of Prose Fiction, with Some Apology for the Fiction of the Author," Bulwer not only applies Schiller's theories to his own fiction, but also makes an important statement about the romance as a narrative convention and about the artistic aims of metaphysical fiction. He claimed that in *Eugene Aram* and *The Last Days of Pompeii* (1834), he had experimented with the dramatic novel mode. Governed by the rules of realism, such novels aimed at presenting a single, unified action; they moved forward through the agency of cause and effect and reached a conclusion without digression or retardation of action.

But to Bulwer the dramatic novel—the realistic novel that came to dominate English fiction after 1840—seemed only a minor form despite its theoretical legitimacy. In contrast, the epic or narrative novel appeared more attractive to his own artistic temperament. Schiller, Bulwer argued, described the epic mode as "ever going forwards and backwards"; its aim was "naked truth," not realism or depictions of outward society.[2] The chief object was "contained in every point of [its] movement; therefore we do not hurry on impatiently towards a goal, but linger lovingly at every step."[3]

The significance of Schiller's theories was that they provided Bulwer with an established narrative tradition in which to locate his own metaphysical fiction, as well as with a means to justify theoretically his movement away from fictional realism. After *Eugene Aram* his novels followed the epic or narrative novel formula. Their metaphysical form arose from his desire not to imitate society, but to "wander from the exact probability of effects" to "bring more strikingly before us the truth of causes."[4] The use of "dim and shadowy allegory," Bulwer believed, distinguished his metaphysical novels from satires, for the metaphysical novel "deserts or resumes" allegory "at will."[5] These novels are neither "wholly allegory, nor wholly matter-of-fact—but both at times."[6]

In his study of metaphysical fiction, Edwin Eigner defines the form as a subgenre of romance, sharing with it many traditional narrative conventions that the realistic novel tried to purify as non-essential after 1830.[7] These impurities—essential points of identification in classifying the metaphysical novel as a type—include "dramatically gratuitous characters, authorial intrusions, episodes, inset stories, digressions, multiple narrators, subplots, and generic contrasts."[8] Further components in Eigner's generic definition are characters who are drawn "on one page as ideal types and on another as realistic portraits."[9] In setting, metaphysical novelists eschewed both "the never-land of their Gothic predecessors" and the realism of "the Dutch-genre-painting world" for what Hawthorne called "a theatre, a little removed from the highway of ordinary travel" with a "suitable remoteness."[10] Structurally, metaphysical novels are divided into two opposing parts, the first presenting a positivist-materialist world view and the second negating this realism with romance. This two-part design creates a pattern of "conversion by contradiction" that allows metaphysical writers to expose materialism and to reestablish metaphysics "as a legitimate province for human inquiry."[11] As Eigner notes, the metaphysical novelists believed that just such a conversion in values was necessary "to the spiritual salvation of their contemporaries."[12]

Godolphin and the Abuse of Ambition and Intellect

In *Godolphin,* his seventh published novel, Bulwer produced a work that took its imaginative source from the fairer fancies and ideal images alluded to in the preface to the 1848 edition of *Paul Clifford.* He composed *Godolphin* simultaneously with *Eugene Aram,* seeing it as an emotional relief from writing about the dark tragedy of Aram's life. The two novels bear a complementary relationship to each other, despite their differences in scene, setting, and character. Bulwer thought them companions because from differing views they attempted to deal with "the frustration or abuse of power in a superior intellect originally inclined to good."[13]

Godolphin appeared anonymously in three volumes in late April 1833 under Richard Bentley's imprint; a second edition, also anonymous, came out in the autumn of 1833. There was much speculation at the time about the book's authorship. Critics attributed it to Mrs. Caroline Norton, Benjamin Disraeli, the late Lady Caroline Lamb, Colonel Caradoc, and the Turkish ambassador. Only *Fraser's,* Bulwer's constant critical adversary, recognized it as his book, claiming in its June 1833 number that Bulwer was "obliged to sneak into the market in a mask . . . to suppress his name in the hope that its absence may contribute to the sale of *Godolphin.*"[14] Whatever the reasons for its anonymity, *Godolphin* never sold as well as Bulwer's other novels.

Dedicated to his friend Count Alfred D'Orsay—"the most accomplished gentleman of our time"—*Godolphin* belongs to Bulwer's series of novels about fashionable life. But unlike his earlier silver-fork novels, *Godolphin* is not intended as a faithful illustration of fashionable society, as it is not composed wholly in the realistic mode. Bulwer felt that its subject—the abuse of intellectual gifts by their misapplication—did not "admit the same facility for observation of things that lie on the surface," but it could lend "itself to [a] subtler investigation of character" and to a closer examination "of some truths . . . worth considering in our . . . social influences on individual conduct" (x–xi).

His artistic aim in *Godolphin* was to trace the abuse of intellect and the waste of talent in a number of representative characters. In the preface to the 1840 edition, Bulwer described his novel's multiple levels of meaning. He saw Percy Godolphin, the hero, in a contrasting, complementary relationship to the hero of *Pelham*. Once all the fopperies, real or assumed, were dispelled, Henry Pelham proved to be the "active man of crowds and cities, determined to succeed," as he is "gifted with the ordinary qualities of success" (ix). In contrast, Percy Godolphin exemplified "the man of poetical temperament, out of his place alike among the trifling idlers and the bustling actors of the world" (xi). Godolphin's social dislocation, Bulwer declared, originated in his "wanting the stimulus of necessity, or the higher motive which springs from benevolence, to give energy to his powers or definite purpose to his fluctuating desires" (ix). In this regard Godolphin is the moral antipodes to Pelham. While possessing higher and richer mental qualities than Pelham, Godolphin evades the struggles of the world and grows indifferent to its duties; he "strives with no obstacles" and "trimph[s] in no career" (ix). To reinforce this theme, the secondary characters grouped around Godolphin—Augustus Saville, Fanny Millinger, and Lucilla Volktman—represent one side or other of Godolphin's dual temperament, either "its conventional elegance of taste or its constitutional poetry of idea" (ix). Yet all are alike in one important respect: each is an example of "gifts misapplied or of life misunderstood" (ix).

Despite its melancholy account of disillusionment, disappointment, and personal failure, *Godolphin* advances a positive argument about the nature of honorable ambition in the temporal world. The book's two leading characters, Percy Godolphin and Constance Vernon, illustrate Bulwer's thesis that ambition is only honorable when it is actuated in behalf of others and when its aim is to raise the fortunes of the human race through benevolence. Constance Vernon's life dramatizes ambition misdirected through ignoble aims and destructive means. Percy Godolphin represents indolence and the pursuit of pleasure. And the Danish sculptor Volktman, who has forsaken his art to devote himself to astrology, exemplifies waste of talent through profitless activity.

Stainforth Radclyffe, a young reform-minded Whig politician, argues the novel's controlling thesis about honorable ambition and public benevolence. He tells Godolphin the proper aim of ambition is service to others. But Godolphin fears that such ambition leads only to perpetual harassments and personal humiliations. Godolphin's energy revives and he enters Parliament as a Tory. His new ambition to be useful leads him to repudiate his long-held doctrines of pursuing the ideal in art and spurning the actual in worldly ambition. He admits to Radclyffe that he was wrong about pleasure. Radclyffe tells Godolphin to look for happiness outside his own narrow notions of pleasure. To do this, he should learn to feel for others and unite himself to a great object. The source of Godolphin's misapplication of intellect, as Radclyffe rightly notes, stems from his essentially poetic temperament.

Writing in 1948, Bulwer's grandson thought that *Godolphin* and its companion novel *Eugene Aram* were the two best-written novels of Bulwer's early works. He claimed that had the reader not known their publication dates, both novels would appear products of Bulwer's later writing career.[15] There is some justice in these remarks. From the view of artistic conception and literary construction, *Godolphin* documents the emergence of the mature novelist, who in this work composed the kind of fiction he always longed to write. Bulwer designed *Godolphin* much as a painter plans a picture, avoiding mere imitative surface and concentrating instead on the presentation of an abstract or intellectual problem elaborated in the novel's overall structure. Modern critic Allan Christensen sees that beginning with *Godolphin*, the element of composition became all-important to Bulwer.[16] Bulwer placed a growing emphasis on patterns of ideas, intellectual concepts, and subtly advanced arguments in which sets of characters and incidents embody the balanced terms and logical divisions of the argument.[17] By combining symbolic meanings and allegorical personifications at nearly every level of *Godolphin*, Bulwer added layers of meaning to his metaphysical vision.

Pilgrims of the Rhine as a "Garland of Wildflowers" Illustrating the Ideal

The Pilgrims of the Rhine was composed in 1832 and belongs to the same period as *Eugene Aram* and *Godolphin*. Delayed in publication until its illustrations could be finished, *Pilgrims* did not appear until early 1834, when Saunders and Otley printed it in one volume. Bulwer dedicated it to his older brother, Henry Lytton Bulwer, to commemorate a pleasant excursion they had shared some years earlier.

Like *Godolphin, Pilgrims* belongs to the ideal and fanciful regions of fiction. With respect to fancy, it may have been too successful, for in the "Advertisement" Bulwer suggested that the book could best be understood if judged by the rules of poetry. From this view, the myths, legends, and superstitions incorporated into the tale fulfill a more recognizable artistic function. In the preface to the 1849 edition Bulwer described the book's artistic aims: it was to be a "collection of the thoughts and sentiments" in the "Romance of Youth."[18] Consequently, the book "has little to do with the positive truths of our actual life" (ix). Its purpose was twofold: to illustrate "visible nature through the poetry of the affections" and to narrate "the most real of mortal sorrows" relieved from pain "by various accessories taken from the Ideal" (ix). The connecting tale, Bulwer claimed, "is but the string that binds into a garland the wildflowers cast upon the grave" (ix).

Travelogue, bildungsroman, fairy tale, and critique of German life, letters, and higher education, *Pilgrims* is unified by Bulwer's dramatization of the ideal. His ten-stanza prefatory poem, "The Ideal World," not only articulates his definition of the ideal, but also provides the frame story and its accompanying seven inset tales with their controlling theme. In the poem Bulwer defines the ideal as "the immortal personifications of all beautiful thoughts" attained either "through the repose of the senses" or in dreams (2). *Pilgrims* focuses on "the diviner love" sought by youth, not attainable in life but achieved in the pursuit of love beyond the world of senses, love that "purifies the soul and awakens genius" (2). Genius, Bulwer argues, in lifting its life to the ideal, becomes itself a pure idea, and by comprehending all existence—all human sins and sufferings—transmutes them. Yet the ideal is not solely confined to poets;

most people, Bulwer believed, could aspire to the ideal through memory, hope, and prayer. In such ways they become poets. Bulwer thought that anyone who rises above his worldly senses in prayer is a poet in his musing with God.

Pilgrims is shaped by two parallel frame stories, one representing the ideal world, the other depicting the actual world aspiring toward the ideal. Both stories are complementary, uniting to create "the outer and the inner world of the land of the Rhine" (12.95fn). The actual-world frame story describes a tour of the Rhine river undertaken by Gertrude Vane and her fiancé Albert Trevylyan. Two patterns of perception and growth shape the young lovers' tour down the Rhine. First is Gertrude's eventual recognition of the fatal nature of her illness and her growing acceptance of death as but a short prelude to her ultimate union of soul with Trevylyan beyond the shore. Second, complementing Gertrude's growth toward the ideal is Trevylyan's alteration in character, marked by his triumph over both self and the sensual aspects of love. Ultimately he separates his ego and sensual nature from a purer feeling for Gertrude. Trevylyan devotes all his energies to make Gertrude's last days on earth a shrine to the beautiful. But at Heidelberg Gertrude falls seriously ill and dies a few days later. Soon after, Trevylyan returns to England, where he throws himself into a life of feverish activity.

Michael Sadleir, Bulwer's most sympathetic modern critic, thought *Pilgrims* "fondent-fiction at its worst, devised for silly girls at Christmas time" and of no greater literary significance than its romanticized engravings.[19] While *Pilgrims* fits some aspects of holiday annuals and prize books, its significance goes well beyond such sentimental literary genres. Part of the book's importance rests on its place among Bulwer's early works shaped by the ideal. But aside from this, *Pilgrims* provides evidence of Bulwer's growing knowledge of German life and letters. Each of the book's seven inset tales carefully imitates several popular German story formulas. *Pilgrims* also presents Bulwer's observations on the development of German literature. He claimed that German literature was too subtle and too homely; its writers did not speak enough to the broad comprehension of mankind. They "turn poetry into metaphysics, and truth seems to them shallow, unless an allegory, which is false, can be seen at the bottom" (18.132).

Ernest Maltravers and *Alice* as Complementary Novels of Apprenticeship to Practical Life

Following the appearance of his two historical romances, *The Last Days of Pompeii* (1834) and *Rienzi* (1835), Bulwer returned to writing novels set in the present day. He published *Ernest Maltravers* in August 1837, and its sequel *Alice; or, The Mysteries* followed in 1838. Both were printed by Saunders and Otley in three-volume editions. In the preface to the 1840 edition of *Matravers*, Bulwer claimed that as a novel of contemporary life, it continued and elaborated on themes found earlier in both *Pelham* and *Godolphin*. He based the novel's philosophical design on Johann Wolfgang von Goethe's *Wilhelm Meisters Lehrjahre* (1796), but he changed the design from an apprenticeship in theoretical art to an apprenticeship in practical life. Bulwer's bildungsroman focuses on a hero who is "not often obstinate in error" but who is "often irresolute in virtue."[20] At times Maltravers is "too aspiring, sometimes too despondent," yet throughout he is subject "to changes of time and fate" (ix–x). He never wantonly rejects the principles Bulwer calls "the science of life"—"a desire for the Good, a passion for the Honest, and a yearning after the True" (x). From such principles experience teaches Bulwer's hero a "safe and practical philosophy," centered on "fortitude to bear, serenity to enjoy, and faith to look beyond!" (x).

Bulwer dedicated his two companion novels to the German people, who seemed to him a race of thinkers and critics, a foreign yet familiar audience "Profound in Judgment, Candid in Reproof, Generous in Appreciation" (i). Technically, *Maltravers* and *Alice* are not exact sequels, as each separately is not a completed artistic whole. *Maltravers* ends abruptly with its central action unresolved; *Alice* continues the action, carrying it forward to its resolution. Together, the two novels constitute a single, unified work, creating a metaphysical vision of life with a complexity of meaning greater than either novel alone.

While *Maltravers* and *Alice* are composite novels with silver-fork, political novel, Newgate novel, and anti-Tracterian formulas at the secondary level, their main principle of organization is the bildungsroman, the novel of self-education. The central action in each novel describes the hero's painful rites of passage as he progresses toward maturity and a hard-won philosophy based on self-knowledge, abandonment of blinding pride, and recognition that love must be the sun of his intellectual universe.

Maltravers provides an account of its hero's boyish errors and wasted youth. In *Alice,* the sequel, Maltravers is thirty-six and still no closer to attaining the grand secret of life. His character remains incomplete; he continues to fall short of his true capacities because of his devotion to a philosophy of indifference and his contempt for ambition. But as *Alice* closes Maltravers finally acknowledges the superiority of love over his vain philosophical quest for the ideal. In Alice's love

[he] found that which shames and bankrupts the Ideal! Here have I found a virtue, that, coming at once from God and Nature, has been wiser than all my false philosophy and firmer than all my pride! You [Alice] . . . have been the example of the sublime moral that teaches us with what mysterious beauty and immortal holiness the Creator has endowed our human nature when hallowed by our human affections! You alone suffice to shatter into dust the haughty creeds of the Misanthrope and Pharisee! And your fidelity to my erring self has taught me ever to love, to serve, to compassionate, to respect the community of God's creatures to which . . . you yet belong![21]

Eventually, Maltravers resumes his public career, this time with far more practical energy than before. His firmness of mind remains, but he no longer despises or condemns humankind by a visionary standard of judgment. As a result of his hard-won experience, Maltravers is far better fitted to mix in the world and to minister usefully to the great objects that refine and elevate humanity. His sentiments, Bulwer's narrator claims, "were, perhaps, less lofty, but his actions were infinitely more excellent, and his theories infinitely more wise" (11.8.445).

Maltravers and *Alice* represented Bulwer's most ambitious and mature writing to date. Critics and readers alike speculated on the degree of autobiographical material shaping each book, especially as Bulwer had claimed that he took much of his tale from everyday life. In his biography of Bulwer, his grandson noted that a good deal of Bulwer's personal experience was worked into the character and philosophy of Ernest Maltravers. Alice Darvil was a further attempt by Bulwer to fictionalize his tragic love affair at Ealing with Lucy D———. Bulwer created Alice as an ideal typification of all that is noble and good in woman, never intending her portrait to be judged solely in realistic terms. Indeed, Alice does not succeed as a fully rounded fictional character. Maltravers, on the other hand, is an impressively drawn character whose long struggle against pride and false philosophy reflects a fairly subtle delineation of human psychology.

The plot of *Maltravers* and *Alice* is more varied and filled with greater movement than any novel Bulwer had previously composed; it unfolds naturally from the circumstances in which the characters find themselves. The scenes and the succession of events are in artistic congruity with the men and women depicted. Bulwer's touches of wit and humor emerge in the play of mind with mind and the friction of wit against wit. Above all, the writing is vigorous and clear, as Bulwer eschewed his earlier stylistic mannerism. Lastly, each novel is filled with a safe and practical philosophy, what Maltravers calls a true science of life, based on a desire for the good, a passion for the honest, and a yearning for the true. These two books are Bulwer's most significant works in the metaphysical mode before *Zanoni* (1842), his greatest achievement in metaphysical fiction.

The Parisians and the Threat of Modern Ideas to Individual Character and National Life

Thirty-five years separate *Alice* from Bulwer's next metaphysical novel of contemporary life, *The Parisians* (1873), his unfinished epic panorama of France set during Napoleon III's Second Empire (1851–70). Between these two novels Bulwer continued writing metaphysical fiction, but it took the shape of occult fiction and historical romances. At the close of his life he returned to composing metaphysical novels of contemporary life; both *The Parisians* and *Kenelm Chillingly* (1873) are products of these last years. These two novels share one element in common: Bulwer's increasing interest in French life and letters. Such an interest is documented in brief passages of narrative commentary scattered throughout *Alice,* where Bulwer argues that French society in 1838 had not kept a balance between the constructive and the destructive principles of society. To Bulwer, already skeptical in 1838 about the social value of the revolutions in France since 1789, it seemed that destruction was fast eclipsing construction in French national life. French literature, Bulwer claimed, contained "a strange mixture of fustian and maudlin," and was, since the rise of Victor Hugo, "fetid, crawling, unformed, and monstrous" (6.2.243). He believed the ruling characteristic of French literature was to take the heart for its story—"to bring the passions and feelings into action, and let the Within have its record and history as well as the Without" (6.2.244). *The Parisians* is particularly interesting because it closely mirrors Bulwer's views about France at the close of his life. If in 1838 Bulwer was concerned about the orientation of French politics and letters, by 1873, when he was an old man alarmed by any form of iconoclasm, he was uncompromisingly hostile to advanced French ideas.

Blackwood's brought out *The Parisians* in four long volumes in 1873, with a prefatory note written by Bulwer's son, the poet-novelist Owen Meredith. About his late father's last writings, Meredith claimed that three—*The Parisians, Kenelm Chillingly,* and *The Coming Race* (1871)—not only were planned and written during the same period but also shared a similar moral purpose. Each was an expostulation against the popularity of modern social and political theories—specifically, Darwinism, democracy, and materialism. According to Meredith, Bulwer envisioned *The Parisians* as a novel of dramatized observation whose artistic aim illustrated the ill effect of modern ideas upon a whole community. Consequently the novel is panoramic in its profusion and variety of scenes and characters. But individually, no one character is more important than any other, as each represents "the impersonal character . . . of the Parisian Society of Imperial and Democratic France."[22] Thus there is no hero or heroine. Bulwer selected French society for his subject because it "was the most advanced in the progress of 'modern ideas' " (vi). The novel, Bulwer's son claimed, represented a long, keen, and practical study of political events, generally acknowledged by many in France as accurate in its assessment of French life and letters (vii).

The Parisians, one of Bulwer's most brilliant but least objective books, is a novel of ideas, or more precisely a novel attacking certain ideas. It is an apologue shaped by his thesis about the forces causing the collapse of imperial France in 1870. Bulwer argues that Napoleon III's glittering and showy imperial system—one that gained France untold wealth at home and great respect abroad—fell because of two dangerous forces from within: materialism and democracy. For Bulwer, January 1870—when Napoleon tried to return to a measure of constitutional rule—not only marked the end of the Emperor's effectiveness as a leader, but prefigured the coming destruction of the imperial system as well. This shift from autocracy to constitutionalism—too much too late in Bulwer's view—demonstrated that Napoleon could no longer rule by the force of his personality. To retain power, he had to solicit personal support from the political parties and a parliamentary system he had longed repressed. He found few to rally behind his tottering regime, however, having alienated so many political factions—the Bourbon and Orleans legitimitists honor-bound to support monarchist pretensions; the old pre-1848 aristocracy who viewed the Emperor as a vulgar upstart; the upper middle classes still loyal to the fiscal policies of the July Monarchy; and the conservative peasantry shocked by the moral decadence of the Imperial Court. In a vain gamble to hold power, Napoleon created a stillborn democratic system by executive fiat and popular plebiscite based on universal suffrage—in Bulwer's view, a rash and dangerous bid for the support of the unlettered and the unwashed. While Bulwer personally advocates France's return to a constitutional monarchy at this point, he indicts those of rank, property, and education for abandoning Napoleon during such a monumental crisis. In the name of both property and civilization, these classes, Bulwer claims, should have closed ranks with Napoleon to prevent the anarchy and destruction that arose from the ill-fated democratic republic and the Commune that preceded the Prussian conquest of France in 1871. Bulwer considers the French defeat by the Prussians a divine punishment for France's impious political and intellectual sins—namely, its experimentation with dangerous modern ideas.

Bulwer dramatizes how the moral cowardice of the propertied classes and the lust for violence and anarchy among the unpropertied may be traced to the effect of advanced ideas on individual and national character. He targets the French intellectuals and literati—especially those who follow the aesthetic doctrines of Victor Hugo—for particular condemnation for helping undermine social stability by their desire to secularize and socialize society. *The Parisians* takes its design from the four groups Bulwer arraigns for their roles in destroying the French social order: the aristocracy for its abdication of political responsibility; the high-finance capitalists for their mammonism and reckless financial speculations; the middle-class men of letters for their betrayal of established moral and artistic standards; and the political radicals for their fanatical pursuit of untried and unsound experiments that strike at the very roots of civilization.

The Parisians concludes with the Prussians at the gates of Paris after Napoleon is overthrown and the Republic is declared. Many of the characters who worked so tirelessly to bring France to its knees are dead, killed either in the revolution or in the Franco-Prussian War. Bulwer intended to end his novel amid the crimes and frenzy of the Commune, planning to show that out of such great evil would come some great good. He believed that in every age, evil or good, a chain of destiny exists that has its roots in "the throne of [the] All-wise and [the] All-good" (2.12.343). In the worst of times some "gleams of prophetic truth" are seen and in such times are "found instincts or aspirations towards some social virtues to be realized ages afterward by happier generations, all tending to save man from despair of the future" (2.12.343). But Bulwer died before he could complete *The Parisians* and indicate what these gleams of truth and redeeming virtues were.

Bulwer's account of how advanced ideas affect French life and individual character is a superb fictional achievement. Written just a few months before his death, *The Parisians* documents both his continued commitment to ideas and his ability to succeed with such a demanding subject despite advanced age and declining health. To the end of his career, Bulwer retained his vigor of mind and his talent for composition and design. In *The Parisians* he denounced what he believed to be dangerous new ideas with the passion of a Hebrew prophet railing against Babylon and Nineveh. Despite his ultraconservative thesis, Bulwer dissected French life and culture with surprising skill and accuracy, providing his readers with a generally well informed portrait of French politics and letters. Whether he was right in claiming that the monarchal principle was a valid political option for France in 1868–71 will never be known, but he was forthright in warning liberals in France and at home about the dangers of unsound and untried political innovations. Bulwer's readers in *Blackwood's Magazine* were sympathetic to his fears that the political dreams motivating socialists and anarchists, if successful, would be the nightmare of civilization. While some may disagree with Bulwer's political thesis, few will fail to recognize that in *The Parisians* he produced one of his best metaphysical novels, one in which each character symbolizes part of the collective French mind.

Kenelm Chillingly and the Pursuit of the Ideal in the Real

Kenelm Chillingly: His Adventures and Opinions, Bulwer's last novel, was completed on the first of January 1873, just a few weeks before his death on the eighteenth of January. *Blackwood's* published it later that year in three volumes, selling 3,150 copies on the first day of its publication.[23] Appraising his father's last writings, Bulwer's son noted that the early satires worked to assail false social respectabilities. In them Bulwer sought to "promote social sincerity and the free play of personal character," while in his later novels he used humor to "protest against the disrespect of social realities," hoping to "encourage mutual charity and sympathy amongst all classes, on whose interrelation depends the character of society itself."[24] In *The Parisians, The Coming Race,* and *Kenelm Chillingly,* however, Bulwer's moral purpose was more definitive and exclusive. In these last three novels he attacked modern ideas that he believed exercised an unwholesome effect on the individual and the community. Such a purpose is worked out differently in each novel. Shaped as a romance, *Kenelm Chillingly* illustrates how a highly wrought imagination stimulated by modern ideas impedes the hero's personal growth and adjustment to society. *Chillingly,* a work of sentiment, is a complement to *The Parisians,* which describes the effects of the same modern ideas on an entire community. But in contrast to *The Parisians,* with its panoramic scope, multiple plots, and large cast of characters, *Chillingly* is a far simpler book, featuring a single plot and a smaller number of characters.

As a metaphysical bildungsroman, *Chillingly* is shaped around a familiar Bulwerian theme: how a brilliant young man of much promise is made indifferent to both ambition and his rightful place in society. This dislocation arises from his superior intellect and from advanced ideas he imbibes that set him apart from others. But through experience, personal suffering, and a tragic but redeeming love affair, Bulwer's hero, Kenelm Chillingly, eventually overcomes his cynical indifference to society. He reaffirms his commitment to the world by discovering that from love and domestic contentment spring all worthy ambitions leading to an active and productive life. This pattern of self-education orders Bulwer's novel, which also provides his final statement about how the real may be achieved, through the ideal. In addition, *Chillingly* is highly autobiographical, as Bulwer once more describes his early love affair at Ealing with Lucy D———. He fictionally reworks this experience, dramatizing a young man's successful reorientation to the world through a commitment to literature. Bulwer's tragic, ill-fated first romance at Grasmere is retold in Kenelm's love for Lily Mordaunt. And through the new ideas that make Kenelm's passage to maturity so painful, Bulwer attacks the social and political theories that he feels weaken a great state. Central to his aim is a condemnation of what he calls the new realistic theology, the new realism in literature, the new politics of downpulling, and the new social phenomenon, E. Lynn Linton's "girl of the period."

In September 1872 Bulwer wrote his friend Mrs. Conway Halliday to apprise her of the progress of *Kenelm Chillingly,* then only two-thirds finished. Its hero, he told her, seems "very strange-humoured" and "original" as a character; the novel, he continued, contains "more poetic bits in it than most of my [other] later writings."[25] Part of this "poetry" was found in Kenelm's adventures and his hopeless love for Lily Mordaunt, as they reflected the author's first boyish romance. Audley Egerton in *My Novel* (1853) expressed Bulwer's nostalgia when he asked, "As we approach death, [do not] all the first fair feelings of young life come back to us mysteriously?"[26] *Kenelm Chillingly* was an old man's book, written by an author who looked back over his life to recapture his first grand passion. The love scenes in the novel embody a sympathetic force, freshness, and sureness of touch, suggesting that Bulwer's own first love had always retained a place in his mind despite a long and busy career.

Bulwer's last completed novel shares with his Caxton novels a common subject: domestic life in the country, featuring everyday experiences and characters attached to the home circle. His prose idyll may be compared favorably to Anthony Trollope's *The Small House at Allington* (1864), for his skill is not far behind Trollope's in providing readers with a slice of domestic life in the provinces. As for his metaphysical novels set in the present, Bulwer completed his apprentice writings with *Godolphin* and *Pilgrims of the Rhine.* *Maltravers* and *Alice* were significant novels displaying his mature powers, but in *The Parisians* and *Kenelm Chillingly* Bulwer produced some of his best work in the metaphysical genre. Yet in his later historical novels and in *Zanoni* he would surpass both *The Parisians* and *Kenelm Chillingly* in the power of his metaphysical vision and in the consummate mastery of his compositional skills.

Chapter Five
Historical Novels and Costume Romances

During Bulwer's lifetime the historical novel achieved immense prestige. Its success was due to Sir Walter Scott's Waverley novels, which determined both the historical novel's essential design and its standard performance. Scott's Victorian successors saw historical fiction as the equivalent of the epic in prose fiction, the most sublime achievement attainable in the novel. To Archibald Allison writing in *Blackwood's Magazine* in 1845, the historical novel was "a delightful and instructive species of composition" because it united "the learning of the historian with the fancy of the poet"; it taught "morality by example" and conveyed "information by giving pleasure."[1] He went on to praise the genre for combining the charms of imagination with the treasures of research. Yet few Victorian historical novels attained many of these lofty attributes; most were merely sensational potboilers and fussy antiquarian costume romances.

In 1846 critic G. H. Lewes complained in the *Westminster Review* about the artistic mediocrity of historical fiction written after Scott's death. Many of these novels published in the 1840s were composed to fit a commercial formula. Lewes explained how to mix the necessary ingredients: "Sprinkle largely with love and heroism, keep up the mystery overhanging the hero's birth till the last chapter; and have a good stage villain, scheming and scowling through two volumes and a half, to be utterly exposed and defeated at last—and the historical novel is complete."[2] This satirical recipe documents something more than a disparity between the artistic ideal and the commercial reality in historical fiction. It provides evidence of the existence of two major divisions in nineteenth-century historical fiction: the historical novel and the historical romance.

The two genres share similar outward characteristics. Each typically features actions set at least forty to sixty years in the past, real historical persons in the plot, and fairly realistic backgrounds.

But the historical romance is determined by sensational and romantic plot requirements (as Lewes described) in which the action turns solely on made-up incidents. History serves only as a painted backdrop, enabling the historical romancer to justify the use of period manners, speech, and colorful costumes—hence the name costume romance. In contrast, the serious historical novel is shaped by a historical thesis, dramatizing how the forces at work in a particular period act to change public and private life. Like an academic historian, the historical novelist is concerned with historical causation, effect, and significance. He can account for social change and explain to his readers even comparatively recent changes. Andrew Sanders argues that through the historical novel "the past could be seen to reflect the present, and . . . modern problems could be judged more detachedly for being considered within a historical perspective."[3]

Bulwer had fairly well defined notions about historical fiction. While he acknowledged Scott's genius and his many contributions to the genre, Bulwer criticized him for treating his historical sources cavalierly, dwelling too much on mere picturesque effects, and having no real grandeur of artistic conception. His execution, Bulwer claimed, was superior to his conception, and Scott never seemed willing "to render palpable and immortal some definite and abstract truth."[4] Writing in the *Monthly Chronicle* in 1838, Bulwer declared that the historical novelist must have "a perfect acquaintance" with the characteristics and spirit of the past. He should "avoid all antiquarian dissertations not essentially necessary to the conduct of his tale" as "minuteness is not accuracy."[5] The novelist's true art, Bulwer continued, "will be evinced in the illustrations he selects, and the skill with which they are managed."[6] Historical novelists, Bulwer advised, who follow Scott must "deeply consider all the features of the time, and select those neglected by his predecessor;— [one] would carefully note all the deficiencies of the author of *Kenilworth* [Scott], and seize at once upon the ground which [Scott] . . . omitted to consecrate to himself."[7] Bulwer's first attempt at historical fiction was his 1829 novel *Devereux,* which, the product of a young writer still struggling through his literary apprenticeship, proved only partially successful. Bulwer did not return again to historical fiction until 1834, when he produced his best known novel, *The Last Days of Pompeii.*

The Last Days of Pompeii: Historical Catastrophe Romanticized

Both *The Last Days of Pompeii* and *Rienzi* (1835)—Bulwer's costume romance and his historical novel set respectively in ancient and medieval Italy—date in conception to the period 1832–33 and were inspired by his visit that winter to Rome and Milan. The idea for *Pompeii* originated in a painting he saw on exhibition at the Brera Gallery in Milan titled "The Last Days of Pompeii," which depicted the destruction of ancient Pompeii in 79 A.D. by the eruptions from Vesuvius. The image of Pompeii's destruction led Bulwer to Naples, where he met Sir William Gell, the respected antiquarian, who guided him in his research of Pompeii. Visiting the site of Pompeii—rediscovered in 1750 and only partially excavated in 1832–33—Bulwer witnessed the recovery of Sallust's mansion, buried for centuries beneath volcanic ash and lava. The bodies exhumed that day Bulwer brought back to life in his imagination, introducing them in his novel as Burbo, Calenus, Diomed, Julia, and Arbaces. Laying aside his incomplete manuscript of *Rienzi,* begun in Rome, Bulwer wrote nearly the whole of *Pompeii* in Naples during the winter of 1832–33.

Bentley published the completed novel in three volumes in July 1834, bringing out several additional impressions that year. Later it was reprinted in a one-volume edition in *Bentley's Standard Novels* in December 1839, as number seventy-two in the first series. Bulwer dedicated the first edition to Sir William Gell in appreciation of his assistance with the book's background sources and as a tribute to Gell's popular books on Roman antiquities. *The Last Days of Pompeii* became an immediate commercial success, creating a greater sensation with the reading public than any other novel since the publication of Sir Walter Scott's *Waverley* in 1814.[8] James C. Simmons is probably right in his claim that the great popularity of Bulwer's novel was due in part to its appearance the same year as the most destructive eruption of Vesuvius in centuries.[9] *Pompeii* has remained in print since its first appearance, becoming Bulwer's best-loved novel. It provided the subject for an opera *(Ione),* numerous stage productions, and eight film versions from as early as 1898 to as recent as 1983.[10]

In the preface to the first edition of *Pompeii,* Bulwer set forth the book's artistic aims. Aside from his interest in the catastrophe that destroyed Pompeii, he was fascinated by the time period—"the first century of our religion and the most civilized period of Rome."[11] From such ample materials he selected "those most attractive to the modern reader,—the customs and superstitions least unfamiliar" to the public (viii). He preserved the symmetry of the novel by resisting the temptation to depict "the hollow but majestic civilization of Rome" (ix). Instead Bulwer confined his story to the destruction of Pompeii, focusing on the "ordinary incidents of life"—the passions, crimes, misfortunes, and reverses of its inhabitants (x). He gave a clue to his artistic intentions, arguing that "we understand any epoch of the world but ill if we do not examine its romance," for "there is as much truth in the poetry of life as in its prose" (x).

Ancient Pompeii, Bulwer claimed, supplied him with the characters best suited to his subject and scene. From Pompeii's connection with the half-Grecian colony of Hercules came the idea for the characters of Glaucus and Ione, the novel's hero and heroine. The Egyptian wizard Arbaces, his base agent Calenus, and the fervent Apaecides arose from Pompeii's commercial trade with Alexandria. Olinthus, the fanatical Christian, was inspired by the early struggles of Christianity at Pompeii. And the blind slave girl Nydia was suggested to Bulwer by a friend, who speculated on the advantages a blind person might have in escaping Pompeii in the utter darkness caused by Vesuvius's eruptions. From his studies of ancient Pompeii, Bulwer strove to recreate an accurate portrait of its manners and customs set in the era of the emperor Titus. But more importantly, he sought a universal theme based on a "just representation of the human passions and the human heart" whose "elements in all ages are the same" (xiii).

The Last Days of Pompeii is a historical costume romance; it is not shaped by a historical thesis or by any serious attempt to identify the historical forces changing public life in the Roman Empire. Romance and sensationalism, rather than historical analysis, give the book its shape and power. Its component parts—catastrophic disaster story, love and murder stories, occult thriller, revenge and fatal prophecy stories, and apology for the sectarian sternness of early Christianity—document Bulwer's artistic aims for the novel. The central action in *Pompeii* focuses on Arbaces' plots to forcibly secure Ione's love and to destroy both Glaucus and Apaecides. Arbaces frames Glaucus for Apaecides's murder, abducts Ione, and hands Glaucus over to the senate for trial. The novel reaches its dramatic climax in the famous arena scene in which Arbaces is exposed as Apaecides' murderer. At that point Vesuvius erupts, spewing forth a gigantic cloud shaped like a pine tree. Blue volcanic lightning illuminates the darkened sky, the earth trembles, and the spectators at the arena are seized with panic. All forget about Glaucus and Arbaces in their frantic efforts to escape to safety. Sallust and Glaucus go to Arbaces' villa and free Ione. En route they meet Arbaces, who demands that Ione be surrendered to him. As Glaucus resists, lightning brightens the sky, showing a large bronze statue of Augustus directly behind Arbaces. Suddenly the earth quakes and shifts, causing the statue to topple forward onto Arbaces, who is crushed beneath it. Eventually, Glaucus and Ione reach the port and safety.

Bulwer's novel closes in 89 A.D. Glaucus is married to Ione and living happily in Athens. He writes to his friend Sallust, telling him that both he and Ione have embraced Christianity, which gives a new dimension to their love for each other. Glaucus's conversion to Christianity is important because it reflects Bulwer's attitudes about both the early Christian church and the evangelical movement in nineteenth-century England. Bulwer depicts the early Christians as stern, doctrinaire, dogmatic, narrow-minded, bigoted, and joyless. They are called atheists by the Romans, who believe that the Nazarenes have rejected all deities. The Christians seem a dread sect; it is believed they always commence their religious rites by murdering a newborn child. Bulwer's narrator notes that the early Christians isolate themselves from others on religious principle, believing that non-Christians are servants of evil, false gods. Such notions lead to the separation of fathers from sons and brothers from sisters, as Christians reject their relatives who retain belief in the traditional deities.

Bulwer claims this fervor was necessary to the triumph of the early church. Its fierce zeal, fearing no danger and accepting no compromise, "inspirited its champions and sustained its martyrs" (2:4.1.35). Bulwer notes that "in a dominant church the genius of the intolerance betrays its cause; in a weak and a persecuted church, the same genius mainly supports [it]. It was necessary to scorn, to loath, to abhor the creeds of other men, in order to conquer the temptations which they presented; it was necessary rigidly to believe not only the Gospel was the true faith, but the sole true faith that saved, in order to nerve the disciple to the austerity of its doctrine, and to encourage him . . . [to convert] the polytheist and the

Heathen" (2:4.1.35–36). The sectarian sternness that confines virtue and heaven to a chosen few supplies the early Christian by its very intolerance with his best instruments of success. It leads the non-Christian, Bulwer argues, to imagine that "there must be something holy in a zeal wholly foreign to his experience" (2:4.1.36). But the same fervor that made "the churchman of the middle age a bigot without mercy, made the Christian of the early days a hero without fear" (2:4.1.36). Bulwer's historical qualification about zeal is important. What is proper to Christian survival at Pompeii in 79 A.D. may not be laudable in England in 1834. Because of the new sectarian zeal of the Low Church faction, the strictness of the growing Sabbatarian movement, and the smugness of the new morality of the 1830s, Bulwer felt compelled to speak out against the increase of religious sectarianism and doctrinal intolerance. Like Dickens and Wilkie Collins, he opposed the more extreme manifestations of the evangelical revival that prized zeal over kindness and correct doctrine over Christian charity. To Bulwer, moderation offered the best protection against the perils of sectarian divisiveness and evangelical enthusiasm. [12]

Pompeii was written expressly to please the public, though Bulwer feared its "elaborate plots and artful management" might not appeal to his female readers. [13] The book's commercial virtues stemmed from its sensational subject, its traditional romance formulas, and its exciting narrative pace. Bulwer showed restraint in his treatment of Pompeii's destruction, effectively placing it at the novel's finale—chapters 4 through 10 in book 5, featuring nearly twenty-five pages of sustained narrative description. He wisely chose not to overemphasize the book's dramatic irony—from the start the reader knows Pompeii will be destroyed—and employed only a few hints of foreshadowing in the book. The artistic effectiveness of these descriptive scenes may have prompted Dickens to incorporate similar ones in *Barnaby Rudge* (1841), in which he vividly described the destruction of Newgate Prison during the Gordon riots. Response to *Pompeii* proved quite favorable. Isaac Disraeli wrote Bulwer that *Pompeii* was the most interesting book published in years. [14] The poet Felicia Hemans thought the novel revealed a higher art in its conception than anything Bulwer had given the public before. It reminded her of the spirit of Goethe and of the great English dramatists of the past. [15] And Lady Blessington believed *Pompeii* contained more true poetry than fifty epics, stamping its author as a genius par excellence.

The book, she wrote Bulwer, was read and universally praised by all. [16]

Rienzi and the Carlylean Hero in Advance of the Age

The resounding success of *Pompeii* encouraged Bulwer to finish the manuscript of *Rienzi*, which had been set aside in favor of other literary projects since his return from Italy. Despite a busy session in Parliament and growing discord with his wife, Bulwer completed *Rienzi; or, The Last of the Roman Tribunes* in November, enabling Saunders and Otley to publish it on 1 December 1835 in three volumes. He dedicated the novel to Alessandro Manzoni. Originally Bulwer had planned to write a nonfiction biography of Nicola di Rienzi, the remarkable fourteenth-century Italian political reformer, because he felt modern historians had judged Rienzi and his era only superficially. But he abandoned this idea, and turned the biography into a work of fiction. In his novel Bulwer took a radically different view of Rienzi's career than was found in Gibbon and Sismondi's standard histories. This was warranted, Bulwer claimed, "not less by the facts of History than [by] the laws of Fiction." [17] In the preface to the first edition of *Rienzi*, he asserted that his biographical novel "adhered, with a greater fidelity than is customary in Romance, to all the leading events of the public life of the Roman Tribune." (viii). Alluding to Mary Russell Mitford's popular play, *Rienzi; A Tragedy* (1828), Bulwer contended that his novel presented a more comprehensive account of Rienzi's life than did any other book in English. As his novel treated the whole of Rienzi's career, he thought it belonged rather to the epic than to the dramatic school of fiction.

Bulwer described his approach to historical fiction in the preface to the 1848 edition of *Rienzi*. His novel's popular success, Bulwer said, came from his reliance on historical facts rather than fancy. Both his plot and characters closely followed historical accounts of the age. He sought to reinterpret these sources and to trace "the causes of the facts in the characters and emotions of the personages of the time" (xi). Bulwer reconstructed the inner psychological lives of actual historical characters, making *Rienzi* a "chronicle of the human heart" (xi). By such invention, Bulwer believed, he created a new harmony between character and event. He found a "completer solution of what is actual and true" by speculating on "what is natural and probable" (xi). These speculations, Bulwer argued, were not "the province of history" but belonged instead "to the philosophy of romance" (xi). In depicting the inner being, Bulwer allied himself with Thomas Carlyle's view of history. Carlyle saw history primarily as biography—as the study of the private and public worlds of the hero, who shaped great events through the force of his personality. With respect to the protagonist, Bulwer's method departed from Scott's formula when he used an actual historical figure as the hero of his novel. Scott, in contrast, had employed fictional heroes, who, representing society and the spirit of moderation, acted as neutral observers of the contending forces of historical change. Bulwer went beyond Scott in another respect when he insisted that historical sources should play the central role in determining the historical novel's content.

Rienzi, unlike *Pompeii,* is a serious historical novel shaped by Bulwer's analysis of the historical forces convulsing fourteenth-century feudal Italy. The novel's controlling thesis is that Nicola di Rienzi, the book's hero, is a political genius hopelessly in advance of his time. The son of an innkeeper and washerwoman, Rienzi rises to supreme political power in Rome in 1347. He quells the violence of the feudal barons, suppresses the foreign freebooters ravaging the roads to Rome, establishes wise and just laws for the Roman people, arbitrates between princes and kings, becomes the idol of the Roman masses, acts as a special envoy of popes, and seeks to unite all Italy as a nation-state independent of the German Empire. His defeat— papal excommunication, loss of office, imprisonment, and assassination—does not stem from his character flaws (pride, insolence, and love of ostentation), but from the spirit of the age. Rienzi's brilliant political skills, powerful intellect, penetrating vision of the future, and inherent love of political moderation are out of character in an age too eager to practice guile, deception, treachery, revenge, and violence—the common political vocabulary of feudal Italy.

Rienzi fails also because he tries to raise the common people of Rome to political supremacy in order to check and moderate the rival powers of the church, the feudal barons, and the German Emperor at Prague. But lacking Rienzi's vision, the Roman people prove fickle, ignorant, and greedy because they are incapable of self-sacrifice, unable to judge events except by outward show and spectacle, and unwilling to support their own newly won political freedoms. Too long oppressed by feudal institutions, the people betray Rienzi at the moment he most needs their continued support to retain power. Rienzi, Bulwer concludes, is too much in advance of his age and too good for the base Italian people. Had he succeeded in all his plans, feudalism might have been replaced by a new era of democratic self-rule and national independence, enabling Italy to avoid nearly five hundred years of disunity and foreign domination.

In appraising Rienzi at the close of his career, Bulwer argues that he exhibits no unnecessary ostentation, indulges in no bouts of intoxicated pride, and commits no single error in policy. He is frugal, provident, watchful, and self-collected. Concentrating every thought on Rome's needs, he "indefatigably . . . inspected, ordained, and regulated all things, in the city, in the army, for peace or for war. But he was feebly supported, and those he employed were lukewarm and lethargic" (2:10.6.227–28). Yet with all his faults, real and imputed, no single act of dark Machiavellian policy ever advances his ambition or promotes his security. Whatever Rienzi's mistakes, Bulwer argues, "he lived and died as becomes a man who dreamed the vain but glorious dream that in a corrupt and dastardly populace he could revive the genius of the old Republic" (2:10.6.228).

Bulwer also attacks modern historians—especially Gibbon and Sismondi—for their biased interpretations of Rienzi. These men, Bulwer complains, regard human beings as if they are machines. They "gauged the great, not by their merit, but [by] their success; and . . . censured or sneered at [Rienzi] . . . where they should have condemned the people (2:9.4.187). Had but half the spirit that motivated Rienzi been found in Rome, the "august republic, if not the majestic empire, of Rome, might be existing now" (2:9.4.187).

Many years after the appearance of *Rienzi,* Richard Wagner told Bulwer's son, then an attaché at Vienna, that his first opera, *Rienzi* (1842), "was the direct outcome of Bulwer's romance of the same name."[18] Of the many letters of praise Bulwer received about *Rienzi,* the most satisfying one came from Albany Fonblanque, editor of the *Examiner,* who thought Bulwer in *Rienzi* equalled Scott in his management of incident and dramatic situation.

Such praise compensated for several unfavorable reviews and charges that *Rienzi* was thinly disguised radical propaganda.[19] These charges

arose from Bulwer's expression of sympathy for Italian self-determination in the preface to the 1848 edition of *Rienzi*. He had
predicted that either Naples or Sardinia might take the lead in
uniting Italy. Yet he cautioned his Italian readers that in shaking
off Austrian control they might find a worse prospect for freedom
in the violence and bloodshed needed to separate Italy from the
sway of her German Caesar. The *Conservative Magazine,* with little
justice, suggested in its review that in *Rienzi* Bulwer forecast the
coming role he meant to play in English politics.[20]

Leila and *Calderon* as Sensational Romantic Potboilers

Leila; or, The Siege of Granada and *Calderon the Courtier* came out
together in one volume under Longman's imprint in 1838. *Calderon*
also appeared by itself the same year in an American edition published by Carey, Lea, and Blanchard of Philadelphia, an American
publisher that specialized in reprinting English fiction. Both titles
were popular with the public; each was reprinted later in Routledge's
Yellowback Railway series (1855) and in Newnes's Penny Library
of Famous Books (1899). Neither *Leila,* a novella, nor *Calderon,* a
long short story, represents Bulwer's historical fiction at its best.
Bulwer intended them as loose thematic complements to each other.
Both employ Spanish settings, treat real historical events, describe
the Inquisition, and feature protagonists driven by revenge and lust
for power—Almamen the Enchanter and King Ferdinand in *Leila*
and Roderigo Calderon and King Philip IV in *Calderon*. While each
story employs one element from Sir Walter Scott's historical novel
formula—a society poised on the brink of great change—neither
is an example of serious historical fiction. Both are shaped by traditional romance formulas—stories about fatal destiny, changelings,
forbidden love, persecuted lovers, and Byronic heroes with unsavory
pasts. At the secondary level both stories use elements taken from
the eastern tale, the occult story, and the gothic romance.

In dedicating these companion tales to his old friend Marguerite,
Countess Blessington, Bulwer lamented that he had not found a
"More Durable Monument" on which "to Engrave A Memorial Of
[their] Real Friendship."[21] Set in 1491–92, *Leila* describes the fall
of the last Moorish kingdom (at Granada) in Spain, destroyed by
the machinations of Ferdinand of Aragon and his éminence grise,

Tomas Torquemada. Bulwer shows little sympathy for either Spaniard and is less than enthusiastic about Ferdinand's restoration of Spanish political hegemony in old Moorish Spain. Ferdinand is drawn as the very soul of deep craft and unrelenting will, a man ruthless, cold-blooded, imperious, and haughty. Bulwer treats Queen Isabel more kindly. She is gifted and high-minded; her virtues are her own and her faults reflect the age in which she lives.

Bulwer based *Calderon the Courtier* on two literary sources: Teleforo de Trueba's *The Romance of Spain* and the elements found in Spanish comic drama. The latter, according to Bulwer, achieved its artistic power by "the prodigality of intrigue and counterintrigue upon which its interest is made to depend."[22] Furthermore, Spanish comedy faithfully mirrored Spanish life, especially in the circle of the royal court. Here, Bulwer claimed, men "lived in a perfect labyrinth of plot and counterplot, [for] the spirit of finesse, manoeuver, subtlety, and double-dealing pervaded every family" (5.319). No house remained free from internal division.

Bulwer's tale is set in the Spain of Philip III, who is a weak, indolent, and superstitious monarch. His kingdom is managed by the Duke of Lerma's political administration. But Lerma—a man mild, ostentatious, and shamefully corrupt—is easily controlled by an upstart courtier named Roderigo Calderon. Calderon's office as Philip III's secretary rests on his willingness to pursue a policy of religious persecution. The plot revolves around Calderon's rivalry with the Duke of Uzeda (Lerma's son), who schemes to supplant both his father and Calderon through his manipulation of Philip III's son, Prince Philip. But Calderon suffers defeat at the hands of his rivals. Imprisoned and tried by the Inquisition, he is found guilty, condemned to death, and publicly hanged.

A hastily written story, *Calderon* is a costume romance and romantic potboiler built only on stirring incidents and melodramatic plot fillers. Bulwer does not analyze the historical forces at work in Spain under Philip III, but focuses instead on romance. In construction *Calderon* is both superficially conceived and shoddily executed. Aside from Calderon, the protagonist, the other characters are drawn with little care or complexity. Most are pasteboard figures common to melodrama. The tale is uncharacteristic of Bulwer's writings as it does not treat his usual theme of the ideal and the real.

The Last of the Barons: The Carlylean Hero out of Step with the Age

In the eight years between *Rienzi* and *The Last of the Barons,* critics attacked Bulwer for making crime appear attractive and showing undue sympathy for criminals in his Newgate novels. He had already published three of his four Newgate romances when *The Last of the Barons* came out in February 1843, printed by Saunders and Otley in three volumes. Eight years of abuse from the critics made Bulwer sensitive about his literary reputation. While he took great pains in composing *Barons,* he was not overly sanguine that it would be judged objectively by the critics. Ill health, domestic problems, and overwork also colored his attitude, causing him to consider abandoning authorship. This mood proved but a passing one of artistic self-doubt, yet he felt so strongly that he ended the dedicatory epistle to *Barons* by observing that while the novel was his best, it would probably be the last with which he would trespass upon the public. [23] Yet the epistle also provided ample evidence of Bulwer's continuing enthusiasm for the novel form: it contained a spirited defense of his theories about fiction. Such a commitment to the aesthetics of the novel belied any serious intention on Bulwer's part to retire from authorship.

The 1843 epistle represented Bulwer's most thoughtful views on the historical novel, a field in which he was increasingly recognized as Walter Scott's most serious and talented successor. Bulwer addressed the epistle to an unidentified critic and friend—perhaps the novelist-critic Harriet Martineau—who had long urged him to write a historical novel with an English subject. The epistle afforded Bulwer the occasion both to describe how he composed historical fiction and to take his critics to task for their cavalier approach to criticism. Historical novelists, he argued, can illustrate certain truths denied the historian and aspire "to something higher than mere romance" (v). They can "increase the reader's practical and familiar acquaintance with the habits, the motives, and the modes of thought which constitute the true idiosyncrasy of an age" (v).

Bulwer discovered these motives and modes of thought through a process he called "analogical hypothesis"—speculation about the psychology of actual historical personages. This speculation, if "sobered by research, and enlightened by knowledge of mankind," could

clear up much that were otherwise obscure, and . . . solve the
disputes and difficulties of contradictory evidence by the philosophy
of the human heart" (v–vi).

Bulwer's use of analogical hypothesis in *Barons* gives the novel
its bold controlling thesis. By reading David Hume; John Lingard;
Edward Hall; Sharon Turner, the Croyland historian; Thomas Carté;
Paul Rapin; Thomas Habington; and Majerus, Bulwer sought to
pinpoint the exact time and specific reason Richard Nevile, the earl
of Warwick, turned against Edward IV. The historical records of
this era were few and badly fragmented. Hall and several other
historians suggested that Warwick's sudden rebellion against Edward IV arose from private rather than public policy grievances.
The king, they speculated, may have attempted to seduce Warwick's
youngest daughter, Anne Nevile. Such a personal insult could explain Warwick's change of policy toward Edward IV. This motive,
however, could not be proven. It was when the historical record
remained unclear, Bulwer argued, that "fiction [found] its lawful
province," helping by "conjecture to [connect] and clear the most
broken . . . fragments of our annals" (xix). Where the historian
only hinted, Bulwer as novelist boldly used his poetic insight to
interpret events. Analogical hypothesis enabled him to connect the
fragments and reconstruct Warwick's motivations for his subsequent
actions.

In the epistle Bulwer also expressed the view that composition
was as important as method in shaping historical fiction. He took
care, he affirmed, to create novels that were artistic wholes, harmonious in their parts and unified in their actions. Like paintings,
literature divided its subjects into those that were familiar, picturesque, or intellectual. Bulwer believed *Barons* belonged to the last
category, a class he felt would never be as popular as the other two
because its merits were less obvious to the average reader. Bulwer
argued that a novel should not be judged on "some prominent
character" or "some striking passage," but rather on its "harmony
of construction, on its fulness of design, on its ideal character,—
on its essentials, in short, as a work of art" (xx). Contempoary
critics, Bulwer complained, failed to use even the most elementary
principles of literary art to determine the degree of failure or success
in the works they undertook to judge. To Bulwer, such ignorance
of the rules of art accounted for the violent fluctuations in criticism,
leading "critics to condemn today and idolize tomorrow" (xxi). The

real distinction between low and high art, Bulwer argued, is found in the presence or absence of the ideal. He "who resigns the Dutch art [realism] for the Italian [idealism]" must remain faithful to the theory that finds "in action the movement of the grander passions or the subtler springs of conduct, seeking in repose the colouring of intellectual beauty" (xxi). From such literary principles, Bulwer conceived and composed *Barons*.

Bulwer selected the reign of Edward IV (1461–70; 1471–85) for the subject of *The Last of the Barons* in order to examine a crucial era in English history, one undergoing great political and social transformation. During that period, Bulwer believed, began the policy consummated by Henry VII (1485–1509) in which the old feudal order was broken up and replaced by a new nobility allied with the growing commercial middle classes. In the fate of the hero of the age—Richard Nevile, earl of Warwick, popularly called the king-maker and the last and greatest of the feudal barons—"was involved the very principle of our existing civilization" (vii).

Bulwer envisioned two artistic aims for *Barons*. First, he wanted to describe fifteenth-century England and the passing of the age of feudalism into the age of commercialism. In particular he sought to bring into full view the characters of the principal personages of the time, their motives for public action, the state of the political factions, the condition of the people, and the great issues of the day. To this end, Bulwer made Warwick the symbol of the feudal state in conflict with Edward IV, the opposing symbol of the new commercialism. He wanted to show how a clash between Warwick, representing the past—the age of individual warlords with their personal armies and powerful family alliances—and Edward IV, exemplifying the future—the coming age of printing and steam power—ended in the defeat of the king-maker by the king. Bulwer's second aim was to reveal the character of Warwick and explain why Edward IV's staunchest supporter suddenly took up arms against him in 1470, espousing the cause of the House of Lancaster (Henry VI and Margaret of Anjou), Warwick's lifelong political enemies.

The Last of the Barons is a serious historical novel shaped by Bulwer's thesis that Richard Nevile turns against Edward IV because of a personal affront. Edward's assault on the virtue of Warwick's youngest daughter drives Warwick to depose Edward, force him into exile, and restore Henry VI to the English throne. But Edward IV's return to England and his sudden defeat of Warwick's armies at Barnet end in Warwick's death and Edward's restoration as king. With Warwick's demise comes the downfall of the old feudal order with its powerful baronial warlords. Bulwer argues that Edward's speedy return to the throne is fostered by the new spirit of the age. Warwick and the barons prove to be men out of step with the times. The new era favors commercialism over feudalism, middle-class traders over chivalrous knights, centralized political authority over weak monarchs controlled by baronial king-makers, and peace at home over incessant feudal warfare. In their desire for economic prosperity, increased middle-class social mobility, and domestic tranquility, the English people restore Edward IV to power. By so doing, they ultimately endorse the subsequent Tudor despotism, which, supported by bourgeois traders, acts at the expense of the interests of the aristocracy and the peasantry. Bulwer believes that such a historical decision decreased England's chances for greater freedom of the individual. In exchanging freedom for the law and order imposed by the Tudor monarchy, England embarked upon an era of rule by regulated deceit, cold calculation, rank opportunism, lust for power, and murder honed to a political fine art—what Bulwer calls the new Italian policy.

Near the end of *Barons* Bulwer speculates on what might have occurred in England had the Lancastrian line continued and its political and social policies endured. England, Bulwer argues, might have seen the power of the monarchy limited by the strength of an aristocracy supported by the agricultural population. The great barons "would have secured and promoted liberty according to the notions of a seigneur and a Norman, by making the king but the first nobleman of the realm" (2:11.2.294). Had such a policy lasted long enough to succeed, the "subsequent despotism, which changed a limited into an absolute monarchy under the Tudors, would have been prevented" (2:11.2.294). Religious persecution of the Lollards (early Protestants) might have been avoided, and with it, the delayed historical revenge of the Puritans. Gradually, the political system might have changed monarchy into an aristocratic government, resting upon broad and popular political institutions. As a consequence, the commercial middle classes might have risen more slowly. And they would not have been made "the instrument for destroying [the] feudal aristocracy, and thereby establishing for a long and fearful interval the arbitrary rule of the single tyrant" (2:11.2.295).

Bulwer's vision of a politically concerned aristocracy allied to a loyal and grateful peasantry—an aristocracy familiar "with the wants and grievances of that population . . . willing to satisfy the one [and] redress the other"—speaks especially to the turbulent 1840s (2:11.2.294). In this period of economic distress and laissez-faire indifference to human suffering, many of Bulwer's contemporaries dreamt of an alliance between aristocrat and laborer, aimed in part at mitigating the horrors of bourgeois industrialization. Such an alliance lay at the heart of Benjamin Disraeli's pragmatic Tory democracy and fed the idealism of Lord John Manners's Young England movement, which hoped for a revived feudal alignment of crown, church, aristocracy, town artisan, and agricultural laborer.

Harold, the Last of the Saxon Kings: The Carlylean Hero in Step with the Age

Bulwer completed his next historical novel, *Harold, the Last of the Saxon Kings,* In April 1848, composing it in less than a month. He wrote much of the novel at the home of his old parliamentary friend, Charles Tennyson D'Eyencourt, the poet's uncle, whose library at Bayon's Manor in Lincolnshire contained one of the finest private collections of early English chronicles in Britain. But the book's publication was delayed because of the tragic death of Bulwer's twenty-year-old daughter, Emily, in London on 29 April 1848, from typhus fever. Richard Bentley printed *Harold* in June 1848 in three volumes. Along with Thackeray's *Vanity Fair,* W. H. Ainsworth's *Lancashire Witches,* Anne Brontë's *Tenant of Wildfell Hall,* and Elizabeth Gaskell's *Mary Barton, Harold* became one of the most successful novels of the publishing season. Bulwer dedicated *Harold* to D'Eyencourt in appreciation of his hospitality and enthusiastic encouragement. In the dedicatory epistle to the first edition of *Harold,* Bulwer claimed he had long entertained writing a novel "on an event so important and so national [in subject] as the Norman Invasion," but he had put aside the project because he feared the ordinary reader was not familiar with the characters or events of the era.[24]

In venturing on such new ground, Bulwer sought the proper fictional mode for his national epic, one that would "produce the greatest amount of dramatic effect at the least expense of historical truth" (xiii). He wanted not to turn history into flagrant romance, but rather to extract "the natural romance of the actual history" (vi). The mode he selected—by discovery and experimentation— arose from employing romance to aid history. Bulwer based his narrative solely on authentic chronicles, constructed his plot from actual events, and described both the personalities and struggles of those who were once the living actors in the real drama. The fictitious part of the novel he confined to the inner life of his characters, which was the legitimate province of the novelist. Here he used "the agency of the passions" only so far as "they served to illustrate . . . the genuine natures of beings who had actually lived" (xv). He strove less to portray manners than to draw the great men of the age, showing their motives and policies in an event he thought the most memorable in Europe. In the preface to the third edition of *Harold,* Bulwer set forth the novel's artistic aims. He wished to acquaint readers with the imperfect fusion of the races in Saxon England, familiarize them with the contests of the parties and am- bitions of the chiefs, show the strength and weakness of a kindly but ignorant church, depict a brave but turbulent aristocracy, il- lustrate how an energetic but disunited people lost their national liberty, and contrast these pictures with the vigorous attributes of the Norman conquerors—their energy, guile, higher knowledge, and rising spirit of chivalry. In a word, Bulwer desired his readers to understand the political and moral features of the age in order to comprehend why England was conquered and how it survived the conquest.

   Harold, Bulwer's best historical novel, treats the closing years (1052–66) of Edward the Confessor's reign, from the return of the banished earl of Godwin and his sons to the establishment of the Norman dynasty under William I following the battle of Hastings. As a composite novel—historical novel, panoramic epic of eleventh- century Saxon England, bildungsroman, and romantic tale of fatal destiny and tragic love—*Harold* is shaped by Bulwer's controlling thesis that England falls victim to Norman conquest because the country is intellectually behind the times, socially backward, and politically weakened by both internal division and constant foreign invasions. Everything, Bulwer argues, is worn out in England. With a king (Edward the Confessor) enfeebled and incapacitated by su- perstition, a court exhausted by cabal and treachery, a church de- crepit and neither learned nor brave, a nobility wearing itself away in combative rivalry yet lacking a true martial spirit, a people debilitated by slavery and materialism, and a national defense system both outdated and impotent against foreign threat, England is easily overrun by superior Norman military organization at Hastings.

By contrast, the Normans are led by an energetic and forceful warlord, who has the support of an efficient court system backed by a learned and disciplined church, as well as the aid of a fiercely effective soldiery using the latest techniques of war. Norman society, Bulwer claims, is a garrison state ruled by Spartan ruthlessness and sustained by a repressed peasantry forced to support a conquest-bent nobility. Yet despite their many flaws, the Normans represent the coming age, while the Saxons exemplify the past. In this clash between new and old, Bulwer dramatizes his theory about the nature of human progress. Drawing an analogy between human society and the natural world, he argues that all communities that advance contain, like nature, "two antagonistic powers—the one inert and resisting, the other active and encroaching."[25] If society develops according to natural principles, then change is inevitable and society and its rulers must welcome reform. Old societies can be reborn, however, and *Harold* predicts that England will eventually absorb its Norman conquerors as it did its earlier Danish and Norwegian invaders, so that eight hundred years later Saxon notions of freedom and liberty will become the signal features of modern nineteenth-century England—a nation that need not fear social change at home or revolutions abroad (1848) because of its willingness to embrace reform and to facilitate change (the 1832 Reform Bill).

Bulwer's novel earned the respect of several important contemporary English historians. Thomas Babington Macaulay told him that "he read *Harold* too eagerly for criticism," but believed the book closer to history than romance.[26] Francis Palgrave, the respected constitutionalist on whose research Bulwer drew, "was delighted that his own 'dull prose' should have contributed to the book's admirable poetry."[27] The antiquarian Thomas Wright complimented Bulwer by telling him he "was alone amongst historical novelists"; others who wrote about the past "had never really studied history" and had "perpetuated prejudices of the most vulgar kind."[28] Several years after Bulwer's death, Lord Alfred Tennyson acknowledged his debt to Bulwer's *Harold* as the major source for his own historical verse drama about the last Saxon king.[29] In contrast, critics writing in the major contemporary journals were less impressed by *Harold*. *Fraser's Magazine* approved of Bulwer's historical analysis in

Harold, but condemned its literary style as "incoherent and unbecoming."[30] Appraising Bulwer's novels in 1865, the *Westminster Review* found *Harold* the work of an author whose mind was commonplace.[31] And Andrew Sanders, writing about *Harold* in 1978, felt the book's major flaw stemmed from Bulwer's technique of dispelling the wonder and strangeness of Harold's world. Bulwer, he argued, "never seems to sense that in demythologising his characters, by emphasising the validity of his own historical credentials, he diminishes both their heroism and their humanity."[32] Such a criticism of *Harold* is just.

Pausanias the Spartan: The Carlylean Hero as Tragic Victim

Pausanias the Spartan, Bulwer's last historical novel, was printed in 1876 in one volume by George Routledge and Sons. It was originally begun in 1852, but for a variety of reasons Bulwer was unable to finish it during his lifetime. His son found the manuscript—completed to the middle of the second volume with a brief two-page outline for the third volume—among his late father's papers. Deciding to publish it, he sent the manuscript to the Rev. Benjamin Hall Kennedy, professor of Greek at Cambridge University, to piece together some of its fragments and to authenticate the book's historical accuracy. Consequently, young Lytton dedicated *Pausanias* to Kennedy for his assistance.

In the dedication dated from Cintra on 5 July 1875, Lytton noted that his father planned to focus his novel on Pausanias's career following the Battle of Plataea, when the Spartan regent, as admiral of the combined Greek fleet at Byzantium, was at the summit of both his power and his public reputation. Bulwer sought to examine why as regent Pausanias proved more powerful than the Spartan king. In his novel he wanted to describe the character of a man who "was at one time the glory, and at another the terror of all Greece."[33] His artistic aim was to depict Pausanias as a tragic hero who, driven by lust for power, by love for a woman forbidden him by his country's laws, and by a loathing for the constraints imposed on his liberty by Spartan customs, betrayed Greece to the Persians in order to rule all Hellas under the guise of making Sparta a great imperial power. Such a bold plan rested on the cooperation of others unaware of his scheme who possessed a collective authority far greater than his own.

For domestic interest Bulwer employed the tragic story of Cleon-ice—her accidental murder by Pausanias and her reappearance as a specter haunting the repose of her guilty murderer—to achieve pathos, dark terror, and dramatic effect as well as to shape the fate of the book's misguided hero.

Based on the portion Bulwer completed, *Pausanias* is the best of all his historical novels because he quite successfully portrays both his hero's inner life and the age in which he lives. Previously, critics complained that while Bulwer proved an accurate historian, he failed to bring his heroes fully to life. With Pausanias, unlike Glaucus, Cola di Rienzi, Warwick, and Harold, Bulwer draws a three-dimensional character and illuminates his psychological makeup.

After *Pompeii,* Bulwer's other historical novels displayed a noticeable advance in conception and method. *Pompeii* contained only the most oblique historical analysis; few of his readers recognized that in the scenes of Roman decadence Bulwer sought to portray the hedonism of the English Regency period (1807–20). Far more direct was his analysis of the forces responsible for the rise and fall of Cola di Rienzi. In *Rienzi* Bulwer put into practice his theory that good historical fiction should be founded on accurate historical reconstruction, analysis of causation, and solid interpretation. He challenged conventional accounts of fourteenth-century Italy, producing a revisionist novel that also dramatized issues current in the nineteenth-century Italian Risorgimento. The same fictional concepts were more successfully applied to *Barons* and *Harold,* which earned Bulwer the praise of contemporary historians such as Palgrave and Macaulay. In his last, unfinished historical novel, *Pausanias,* Bulwer overcame his difficulty in depicting the psychological lives of the historical personages in his story, a problem he had not fully resolved in his earlier books.

A modern critic, Lionel Stevenson, has judged Bulwer's later historical novels both "sound and scholarly."[34] If these novels are to be faulted, they may be criticized for being overly self-conscious about method: occasionally Bulwer interrupted his narrative to cite his sources and to acquaint his readers with contending interpretations offered by other writers. This concern for documentation infuriated contemporary critics, who accused Bulwer of parading his knowledge to no useful purpose.

Bulwer's place as a historical novelist remains secure; he was Sir Walter Scott's most important and most serious successor in the early Victorian period. Until the historical novel's return to popularity in the mid-Victorian era, no writer did more to preserve and improve upon Scott's fictional legacy than Bulwer. The other aspirants to Scott's mantle—Harrison Ainsworth, G. P. R. James, Horace Smith, John Gibson Lockhart, and Mrs. Catherine Gore—are long-forgotten today. But Bulwer's historical fiction is still read, and *Barons* and *Harold* retain their power as works of serious historical analysis. Despite their artistic flaws, his historical novels are the link between *Waverley* and *Henry Esmond;* without him the English historical novel might have expired in the 1830s and 1840s from its exploitation by romancers whose hackwork seriously undermined the genre.

Chapter Six
Domestic Novels

Victorian and modern critics agree that in his domestic novels of the 1850s Bulwer reached the summit of his literary achievement. In them he turned away from romance, crime, and adventure and focused instead on the delineation of character and the study of life in more normal surroundings. Bulwer's transition from romantic sensationalist to domestic realist reflected a slow process of personal and artistic evolution during the mid-1840s, one that led him to a new phase in his writings. As his grandson noted, Bulwer's domestic novels are marked by an atmosphere of "quiet serenity" in which "the humour is entirely free from satire, and the characters are at once lifelike and sympathetic."[1]

In the three domestic novels comprising his vastly popular Caxton series—*The Caxtons* (1849), *My Novel* (1853), and *What Will He Do with It?* (1858)—Bulwer attained an unusual harmony between ends and means, between conception and execution, and between ideal and real modes of composition. Further, although these novels were written expressly to appeal to the popular literary market, Bulwer did not feel at the time that he was compromising his aesthetic principles. Rather he believed he had discovered a new artistic vision that united his art with the common concerns of the people. Previously Bulwer had practiced what he called "an Intellectual or unpopularly ideal art," writing for a select and relatively small reading public.[2] But during the 1840s he underwent a genuine change of heart about the craft of fiction, declaring after 1846 that he really held "his soul in common with all men."[3] Instead of writing for a reader ideally like himself, he now strove to write for the mass of ordinary people.[4]

Bulwer's shift from an ideal to a more popular art was reflected in the advice he gave his son about cultivating the popular element in his poetry. Seek, he said, "broad effects, opinions, humours, feelings, [and] thoughts that every man in Oxford St. knows."[5] By addressing the popular element Bulwer did not mean merely pandering to popular literary formulas, but discovering instead the

"expression of a something which comes home to the greatest number of human hearts and souls."[6] This something, he claimed, could
be found only in the "breadth of [character] types" and in "the
pathos of generosity and self-sacrifice."[7]

He elaborated this notion in an essay titled "Faith and Charity,"
which he later reprinted in *Caxtoniana* in 1863. Literature, he wrote,
should cultivate "a visible wisdom of conciliation" in which the
author treats the reader as friend and brother, "seeking to conciliate
our sympathies even where they expose our infirmities."[8] Writers
who employ this wisdom "please us most," causing "us to return"
frequently to their books "as they create agreeable sensations . . .
which reconcile us to life and humanity."[9] In the essay Bulwer
praises Horace for his charm, Cervantes for his kindly laugh, LeSage
for his good-tempered smile, Addison for his common sense, and
Goldsmith for his domestic sentiment. None of these authors spares
human follies or errors, nor do they revile or libel the reader by
their frank, plain-spoken truths. Instead they provide a unifying
sense of cordiality that humanizes their readers through a rhetorical
blend of love, laughter, and constructive criticism.

From these writers Bulwer shaped his own theory of domestic
fiction, one modeled on conciliation and cordiality. Such a theory
advances an essentially comic moral vision of life that bears some
resemblance to George Meredith's Comic Spirit. Like Meredith,
Bulwer sought to heal people of their absurdities and blinding
egoism by demonstrating that, if we are to be whole, we should
possess the capacity to recognize our own follies and laugh at them.
Egoistical idealism must give way to the realities of life if we are
to see ourselves in a more sensible light.

The realism shaping Bulwer's comic vision had its origin in his
changing political philosophy. His Benthamite reformism, Godwinian radicalism, and German philosophical idealism of the 1830s,
the source of much of his fiction, were tempered by political events
both at home and abroad during the 1840s. The selfish irresponsibility of the Manchester school (the Cobdenites), the threat of
violence in English Chartism, and the tragic futility of the continental revolutions (1848–49) led Bulwer to discount the value of
a heroism devoting itself to ideal causes—political nationalism and
the right of self-determination among subject minorities. While he
approved of revolutionaries like Lajos Kossuth and was "quite an
enthusiast" for Garibaldi and Mazzini, Bulwer quickly saw the use-

lessness of their idealistic crusades. [10] Writing of the overthrow of papal rule at Rome (1849), he told his friend Lord Walpole that "I have seen nothing so heroic and with so good a cause; but, alas! so hopeless." [11] Similarly, in England Bulwer grew to distrust doctrinaire idealists, fearing that, whether Chartist or Manchester ideologues, they posed a serious threat to social peace and general well-being. To John Forster he complained about the economic liberals: "Those miserable Cobdens. . . . What fools they are, and these are the men by whom England herself has been half driven to the brink of revolution." [12]

Bulwer's speeches during the 1840s illustrated his new political realism, for their constant theme was how best "to secure in actuality and not merely in theory a House of Commons that would express the common sense of the common interest." [13] For Bulwer, social improvement increasingly became a question of reforming the individual first, a notion foreshadowing his political conservatism of the 1850s. Against a backdrop of the failure of revolutionary movements on the continent, he despaired for idealism and collective political action as useful forces to attain either reform or greater individual liberty. He voiced his disillusionment to Forster in 1849, remarking that "more and more do we see that our only realm of liberty and improvement is our own individual natures." [14]

Converting his political beliefs into fictive art, Bulwer ordered his domestic novels around a recurring theme: how best to improve the individual's basic nature. Unlike his biting satires of the 1820s, where societal improvement stems from public action, his comedies of conciliation (1850s) stress personal melioration through greater self-knowledge. Thus social betterment comes not from an act of parliamentary reform but from an act of private cognition. On this subject, Bulwer wrote Lord Walpole in 1850 that the real secret of the age is "the proper arrangement of one's life into something like orderly method, avoiding the passions, but not the affections, getting rid of false excitements and the necessity of that stimulant—change—whether in persons or things. In short, trying to concenter one's existence so that one might get into the circle the enjoyments most to our individual tastes, and least injurious to other people." [15]

Bulwer's philosophy of life, as expressed to Walpole, is equally descriptive of his theory of domestic fiction. Both eschew passions and false excitements, preferring instead an orderly existence of

innocent pleasures. No better statement could be found to record
Bulwer's transition from sensational romancer to domestic realist.

The Caxtons as a Homily on Common Household Affections

The Caxtons: A Family Picture was serialized in *Blackwood's Magazine* from April 1848 to October 1849 and published in November 1849 by John Blackwood in three volumes. Both the serial and book versions, for which Bulwer received £1,200, appeared anonymously, raising public speculation about the author's true identity. The poet Robert Southey's widow, struck by the novel's similarity in sentiment and style with her late husband's writings, wrote John Blackwood on 24 February 1849 inquiring who was the author of the series "of admirable papers still in course of appearance in Maga?"[16] Had she not known better, Mrs. Southey told Blackwood, she would have ascribed *The Caxtons* to no other pen than Robert Southey's.[17]

The book dates to 1843, when Bulwer simultaneously conceived *The Caxtons* and *Lucretia* (1846) as complementary novels. With half of *The Caxtons* written in 1846, Bulwer set it aside and finished *Lucretia*. He returned to *The Caxtons* in the fall of 1847, completing it in early February 1848. As he observed in the preface to the 1853 edition of *Lucretia,* both books were intended "as pendants . . . to show the influence of home education, of early circumstance and example, upon after character and conduct."[18] The moral design for the two novels was identical, but in *Lucretia* Bulwer sought "the darker side of human nature," resorting to "the tragic elements of awe and distress."[19] In contrast, *The Caxtons* depicted the more "sunny and cheerful" side employing "the comic elements of humour and agreeable emotion."[20] *Lucretia* portrayed the evil, *The Caxtons* the salutory influence of domestic moral training.

In the preface to the first edition of *The Caxtons,* Bulwer claimed his novel should be seen as an experiment quite different from his previous fiction.[21] It represented the first of his works "in which Humor has been employed, less for the purpose of satire than in illustration of amiable characters." It was "the first, too, in which man has been viewed, less in his active relations with the world, than in his repose at his own hearth,—in a word, the greater part of the canvas has been devoted to the completion of a simple Family Picture" (v). As a consequence, the novel expressed "the sympathies

of the human heart" where "the common household affections occupy
the place of those livelier or larger passions" once commanding "the
foreground in [his] Romantic composition" (v). In his hero, Pisistratus Caxton, whose autobiography connects the different characters and events, Bulwer sought to "imply the influences of Home
upon the conduct and career of youth" (v). With respect to the
novel's colonial message he intended his hero to represent a type or
class, exemplifying "the exuberant energies of youth, turning, as
with the instinct of nature for space and development, from the
Old World to the New" (vi). Finally, the novel's interior meaning
was that "whatever our wanderings, our happiness will always be
found within the narrow compass, and amidst the objects more
immediately within our reach"—a hackneyed truth "we are seldom
sensible of . . . till our researches have spread over a wider area"
(vi).

Combining the domestic comedy, the bildungsroman, and the
novel of colonial life formulas, *The Caxtons*—with its large cast of
characters, panoramic view of life, and multiple plots—is an apologue extolling the simple virtues of home and heart. Using a
metaphor of human spiritual progress as the great battle of life,
Bulwer argues that we must cultivate the sanctity and happiness of
self-sacrifice, best done through early moral education at home.

To Bulwer the ideal of home is one in which perfect trust and
truth reside together, a place where the holiness of filial love leads
to exquisite happiness and where families bound by mutual affection
share the cares and duties of everyday life. By fostering the virtues
of love, human sympathy, benevolence, and generosity of heart, we
can discover in life something higher and better than self. Every
desire, every dream of fortune, and every hope of success must be
linked to the concerns of others to find true happiness. Blessed with
these salutary attributes, we can more easily renounce the worldly
passions—egoism, false pride, selfish ambition, and misdirected
desires for wealth and power—found in external things. Such passions only blind us to duty and honor and are but empty prizes in
the great lottery of life, prizes more easily won by sin than by virtue.
We must strive for the greatest moral good on earth, Bulwer claims,
if we are to achieve heaven. By following the divine but visible
principle of good, we can learn to recognize our selfish aspirations
and guard against egoism. For egoism exacts all and resigns nothing,
preventing us from successfuly embarking on our great pilgrimage

in time toward eventual, eternal progress. Moreover, these same
values inform Bulwer's theme about colonial emigration. Home
virtues may be seen as a school from which the broader responsibilities of citizenship arise and spread overseas, uniting home and
empire in a bond of mutual respect and interdependence.

Bulwer subtitled his novel *A Family Picture,* but he meant family
in the plural. *The Caxtons* examines several contrasting families,
showing how home training, circumstance, and parental example
shape the character and conduct of children as they grow into adults.
While all the characters illustrate some aspect of Bulwer's thesis,
none are more central to it than Austin Caxton and his son Pisistratus
(called Sisty by his parents). Both exemplify sound moral values
and serve as a measure against which all the other characters are
judged. From Austin and his wife, Kitty, Sisty receives a solid
moral education that enables him to bear reversals in love and fortune
until he finds ultimate happiness. He succeeds because he is able
to harmonize his moral and intellectual faculties, finding both peace
of heart and peace of mind.

As the narrator of *The Caxtons,* Sisty begins his autobiography
retrospectively, describing his birth and christening in the comic
tradition of Laurence Sterne's *Tristram Shandy* (1760–67). His father, abstracted by his studies into the authorship of *The Iliad,*
absentmindedly names his son Pisistratus after the disputed arranger
of Homer who enslaved Athens six hundred years before the birth
of Christ. When his wife christens the baby after the Greek tyrant,
Austin, outraged, accuses her of making him the father of an anach-
ronism. Such comic scenes indicate Bulwer's debt to Sterne, as do
the characters who are Victorian adaptations of the denizens of
Shandy Hall—Austin is Mr. Shandy, his brother Roland resembles
Uncle Toby, and Doctor Squills approximates Dr. Slop.

In contrast to Austin is his older brother, Captain Roland de
Caxton, a widower with two children and a ferocious devotee of the
code of family honor. He is a one-legged army veteran retired on
half pay who still proudly wears his Waterloo medal. Motivated by
a strong sense of personal honor, Roland believes that courage is
the first virtue honor calls forth and that all society and civilization
proceed from it. Both brothers have bees in their bonnets, but they
dearly love each other. Austin actively works on a multivolume
study called *The History of Human Error,* which is a moral history
espousing the view that only by racial mixing can humanity reach

its destined state of perfection. In temperament Austin is slow and mild, Roland quick and fiery. The scholar reasons while the soldier imagines. Austin's sweetness, polish, and lack of ambition contrast with Roland's sternness, rough manner, and passionate energy.

Both brothers maintain a long-standing quarrel about their family name. Roland insists it originates from Sir William de Caxton, who was killed at Bosworth Field while serving under Edward III. Austin argues that it derives from the great printer William Caxton. After years of contention they have reached a compromise—when Austin visits Roland they believe in the printer; when Roland comes to see Austin they support the hero of Bosworth Field.

Roland's son, Herbert, the novel's Ishmael, typifies worldly ambition and egoism. He dramatizes Bulwer's theme about passion overruling thought and represents the ill effects of a faulty upbringing. Neglected as a child by Roland, harmed by his mother's baleful example, and corrupted by his early education, Herbert grows up a ne'er-do-well who is arrogant, envious, cold, and cynical—the reverse of Sisty, his opposite in the novel. He craves success not to be loved or esteemed, not to serve or shine, but to be able to despise a world that galls his self-conceit and denies him the pleasures of life. His character is ruled by two traits: a keen power of calculation and an unhesitating audacity.

Herbert's formal education in France further undermines his character. His tutor, a rationalist and follower of Voltaire, follows the bias of his pupil's mind in order to bring out rather than thwart his genius. Such a system is anathema to Bulwer, whose narrator remarks that while mind, understanding, and genius are fine things, they reflect a system that ignores the fundamental values of the spirit. Where, he asks, "in all this teaching, was one lesson to warm the heart and guide the soul?" (16.4.97). In addition Herbert reads French novels that corrupt his fancy and confuse right with wrong. Bulwer considered contemporary French fiction bold and energetic but filled with "strange exaggeration . . . mock nobility of sentiment . . . inconceivable perversion of reasoning . . . and damnable demoralization!" (10.1.264). These novels paint society in hideous colors, turning class against class and making roguery both probable and natural. In Bulwer's view they represent the destroying principle in life and unsettle the established moral order. As a result of his education, Herbert grows up with his ambition perverted, his intellect distorted, and his heart twisted.

Unlike Herbert, who is devoted to self, Sisty finds happiness in living for others. His early manhood proves painful: he suffers through a hopeless love for Fanny Trevanion and fails to take his degree at Cambridge because his uncle's reckless speculation ruins the family. To cure his son's romantic malady, Austin prescribes a book titled *The Life of Robert Hall.* Sisty finds much comfort in the book, which preaches the necessity of doing the most good on earth in order to reach a higher existence in heaven. The author urges his readers to follow the divine and invisible principle of good that calls upon us to contemplate the selfishness of our hopes and seeks to awaken us from an egotism that exacts all and resigns nothing.

Despite his reduced prospects, Sisty believes there is much for which to live and strive. He resolves not to suffer the egotism of passion or submit to self-pity. Rather Sisty feels that with hard work he can grow rich and in time retrieve his family's fortune. Action and useful labor will at least silence any thought of Fanny Trevanion. He vows two great objects in life: financial independence for himself and economic security for his family. To achieve them, Sisty decides to emigrate to Australia. Herbert also decides to go out to Australia as he believes the New World a fair field in which to work out his moral reeducation.

Bulwer divided *The Caxtons* into eighteen parts, with the last two set in Australia. These closing scenes afford those characters embarking for Australia a chance to make their fortune and find some form of personal salvation. In addition Bulwer took the opportunity to articulate his ideas for a more active colonial system, policies he later carried out as colonial secretary in Lord Derby's short-lived Conservative government (February 1858 to June 1859). Escott, one of Bulwer's modern biographers, believed that the true cult of the colonies was first sounded in *The Caxtons,* some eight years before Bulwer began to educate his ministerial colleague Disraeli about the necessity of upholding England's empire overseas.[22]

Bulwer saw that the colonies offered not only a remedy for overpopulation but an outlet for surplus intelligence and energy not needed in England. In particular, Bulwer encouraged people of the middle and upper classes to emigrate to the colonies, so that with what he called "the refuse" went people of a better class, blending the aristocratic with the democratic in colonial settlements. It was important that England transplant to her colonies as high a standard of civilization as possible to forge a closer link with the parent state.

Bulwer recognized that someday these settlements would grow into independent states, and that by prudent policies England could lay the seeds now for "a constitution and a civilization similar to our own, with self-developed forms of monarchy and aristocracy, though of a simpler growth" (12.6.353). On the other hand, failure to implement such a policy would raise "a strange, motley chaos of struggling democracy,—an uncouth, livid giant, at which the Frankenstein may well tremble, not because it is a giant, but because it is a giant half completed" (12.6.353). Bulwer remarks that whether "the New World will be friendly or hostile to the Old" depends less on "kinship of race" than on "similarity of manners and institutions" (12.6.353–54).

Sisty sails for Australia, hoping to turn his hardihood, fortitude, and plain common sense to some account. While in Australia, Herbert completes his moral reeducation and wants to join the army to redeem his name. The blot on his name, Sisty tells him, is erased by his manly reform, steadfast industry, and blameless conduct in Australia. All his errors, Sisty continues, arose "from an uneducated childhood and a wandering youth" (17.2.144). He tries to persuade Herbert that there is no greater glory than laying the rough foundations of a mighty state, though no trumpets resound with this kind of victory. But Herbert resolves to enter the army and he goes out to India to join his regiment.

Eventually Sisty returns to England, where he is reunited with his parents. Bulwer ends *The Caxtons* with news from India that Captain Herbert Caxton has fallen in battle; his death at last vindicates his honor. At the Tower, Roland commemorates Herbert's death by erecting a tablet that reads, "He Fell On The Field: His Country Mourned Him, And His Father Is Resigned" (18.8.190). With the triumph of the virtues of home and heart, of conciliation and affection, Bulwer concludes his novel about the great battle of life, in which all men must undergo an earthly probation in their journey to a wiser and better existence.

Bulwer felt that the art he had employed in *The Caxtons* was a simple one within the reach of all. It consisted of creating agreeable emotions and avoiding subtle or deep emotions that might cause pain and uneasiness. In *The Caxtons* he succeeded in showing that he could produce humor without sarcasm and tears without bitterness, following the one literary formula that rarely failed to be popular. The book's calmer atmosphere, greater humor, and clearer expression of human kindness made his literary reputation, giving him an equality of status with Anthony Trollope and the other domestic realists dominating the novel during the 1850s. Certainly few Victorian novels came closer to capturing the spirit of *Tristram Shandy* than *The Caxtons,* for its comic characters genuinely won the public's interest and affection. While not as ambitious as *My Novel* in its scope, *The Caxtons* is filled with solid and useful truths about the family circle and its importance in elevating the moral tone of public life. Its colonial section set the formula for the Australian novel, influencing writers as diverse as Henry Kingsley, Fergus Hume, and Henry Handel Richardson. Bulwer's predictions about the future relationship between England and her overseas possessions proved true. His interest in a revitalized colonial policy was in advance of Gibbon Wakefield's famous system.

My Novel as a History of Contemporary Intellectual Types

The public success of *The Caxtons* assured Bulwer of further opportunities to serialize his fiction in *Blackwood's Magazine,* one of the most prestigious periodicals of the age. This new association proved advantageous to both Bulwer and John Blackwood. In Bulwer, Blackwood acquired for his magazine a popular, best-selling novelist, and in Blackwood, Bulwer had an enlightened editor who gave him shrewd advice and perceptive criticism. As a fairly regular contributor to *Blackwood's,* Bulwer found in its readers a compatible audience whose conservative views roughly paralleled his own on many issues. As Walter E. Houghton has noted, *Blackwood's* championed a semi-feudal society in which a privileged rural landowning class still believed it had certain duties and responsibilities toward the lower social orders. Its editorial policy supported all rural and agricultural interests to the exclusion of urban and industrial concerns. At times *Blackwood's* romanticized a rugged yeomanry and espoused a primitive patriotic jingoism.[23] Many of these notions Bulwer preached in his novels after 1848.

If John Blackwood acted as Bulwer's literary mentor for his next book, *My Novel,* the idea for it originated with another publisher, Henry Colburn. Colburn suggested to Bulwer that the public might welcome "some sketches of . . . polite life, character, and incident" as a contrast to Dickens's stories of humble life, provided Bulwer "suitably connected them" with "a stirring plot."[24] Bulwer offered the completed sketches to Blackwood, who serialized them in *Blackwood's Magazine* in twenty-eight monthly installments from September 1850 to January 1853. In early 1853, Blackwood published *My Novel, by Pisistratus Caxton; or, Varieties in English Life* in four volumes. Bulwer dedicated the book edition to his brother, Sir Henry Lytton Bulwer, for his "services [to] England" and as "a Memorial of Brotherly Affection."[25]

My Novel is the second book in the Caxton trilogy, but it does not feature any of the characters from the first novel in central roles. Sisty, his wife, Austin, Kitty, Roland, and Dr. Squills form only an appreciative chorus in the proems beginning each of the novel's twelve books. They argue about the respective merits of their favorite characters, comment generally on the story's action, and debate what the ultimate significance of Sisty's novel should be. The proem as narrative convention becomes a topic of discussion in the introduction to Book Two. Austin urges Sisty to imitate Henry Fielding's use of introductory chapters at the head of each major division in his own novel—just as Fielding did in *Tom Jones* (1749). These introductions, Austin jokes, are indispensable as they allow the reader the advantage of beginning the novel on the fourth or fifth page rather than on the first. They create contrasts and give the author an opportunity to explain what has gone before and what is yet to come. Proems also introduce light and pleasant ornaments, providing proper places for the reader to pause and reflect on what he has read. Lastly, Austin claims, they invest the whole novel with a fixed design and give it a harmonious ethical department (space for moral commentary). But Sisty worries that authorial intrusions might mar the novel's realism.

These narrative devices establish Bulwer's literary debt to Fielding. The prevailing tone and the country-life atmosphere in *My Novel* led Ernest A. Baker to suggest that Bulwer's novel might be seen as a Victorian parody of *Tom Jones*. Squire William Hazeldean, he noted, "has more than a spice of Squire Western";[26] Leonard Fairfield, the book's hero, is another Tom Jones; Randal Leslie plays a suitably wicked Blifil; Jemima Hazeldean suggests Bridget Allworthy; Riccabocca, the exiled Italian count, is Partridge; and Audley Egerton, the high-souled politician, resembles Squire Allworthy.[27] But such comparisons should not be pushed too far, for Bulwer's aims in *My Novel* are quite different from those Fielding entertained in *Tom Jones*.

My Novel is written in part to secure the triumph of what Bulwer calls sound principles. As a romance of real life, the novel treats familiar scenes and seeks to rehabilitate (in unsettled times) the reputations of both the country squire and parson, traditional symbols of rural authority. Bulwer, however, has no interest in drawing the old-fashioned squire and parson of Fielding's day. Instead he focuses on their present-day types. In this way he hopes to "do something useful" in "a few good-humoured sketches" to encourage the public to rightly view these "innocent gentlemen" in proper perspective (1:1.1.6). There is a need for these sketches, Bulwer claims, as "many popular writers are doing their best, especially in France, and perhaps a little in England, to set class against class" by picking "up every stone in the kennel to shy at a gentleman with a good coat on his back" (181.1.6). He hopes to show that those of the rural ruling classes, however much they may be disliked, are really little better off than their neighbors. But given the present state of society, Bulwer says, "we shall all have to endure" the system as constituted, for it is "as good . . . a [one] as we are likely to get, shake the dice-box of society how we will" (1:1.1.6).

A long book totaling 1,424 pages in its first edition, *My Novel* is composite in design, being part bildungsroman, part political novel, and part metaphysical novel of ideas. Bulwer classified it in Fieldingesque terms as "a humble familiar epic" and "long serio-comedy" with a large cast of characters who belong to "that species which we call Intellectual" (1:8.1.184). His novel, the best of the Caxton series, mounts a metaphysical inquiry into the intellectual life "of our passing generation," illustrating the deficiencies that "mere intellectual culture leaves in the human being" (1:8.1.184).

In particular, *My Novel* investigates the ill effects of both the Manchester school (laissez-faire capitalists) and the French school (radical democrats and iconoclastic novelists) on contemporary (pre–1832 Reform Bill) English society. Advancing the views of left-wing Toryism, Bulwer attacks both schools for being part of the destroying principle pushing civilization into the abyss. To combat such social divisiveness, he argues in behalf of what he calls the unifying sentiment of cordiality, which reconciles contending classes and acts as the vital principle of civilization. His aim is to balance liberty with order and to reestablish the old English feeling of congeniality between classes. The sentiment of cordiality finds its best expression in Bulwer's doctrine of sympathy—man's capacity to feel joy and sorrow not in himself alone but in common with those around him. Nature, he argues, implants sympathy as a human instinct and Christ exalts it as a command. Rich and poor alike must have sympathy and toleration for each other, for by bearing one another's burdens, we fulfill the law of Christ. He who only feels for himself abjures his very nature as man. Sympathy, joy, and common suffering "connect the family of man into one household" and "by such feelings is man distinguished from . . . brute creation" (1:2.12.146).

Ernest A. Baker observed that while the multiple plots in *My Novel* were brilliantly conducted, they set the reader "doing cat's-cradles" and "puzzling his brains."[28] But this bewilderment arises not from the magnitude or intricacy of the novel's four main plots—the Lenny Fairfield, Randal Leslie, Frank Hazeldean, and Audley Egerton/Harley L'Estrange plots—but from its metaphysical design. *My Novel* is less a fictitious history of real life than an intellectual puzzle whose characters represent types and whose central actions become emblematic of a secular *Pilgrim's Progress*.[29]

Bulwer classified such literature as stories with double plots, but he did not mean plot in the conventional sense described by Aristotle in *The Poetics*. Rather, he referred to a "duality of purpose" that combines "an interior symbolical signification with an obvious popular interest in character and incident."[30] The cat's-cradle Baker spoke of can be unraveled and made clear by identifying the novel's central types, symbols, and emblems. All four plots chronicle the spiritual progress of the characters as they attempt to pass from life integral (the ideal and the visionary) to life fractional (the real and the actual). Those characters actuated by the attributes of the heart survive their ordeal, becoming psychologically and spiritually whole; those motivated solely by the values of the head, unless converted by heart, are destroyed during their quest.

Lenny Fairfield, the novel's moral hero, symbolizes the union of intellect with conscience in his rise from unlettered peasant to poet and practical inventor. As poet (the visionary) and inventor (the actual), he is a synthesis of heart and head and attains a balance between the ideal and the real. Because he is able to replace his youthful alienation and rebellion with patience, abnegation of self, pride devoid of egotism, and faith in personal improvement, he also exemplifies the triumph of sound principles.

Parson Dale, who symbolizes sound moral values, articulates part of the novel's controlling thesis, especially in his comments about human sympathy. He argues that God made human beings unequal in worldly possessions and burdens as a test (spiritual probation) for heaven. Both rich and poor, he exhorts, should show sympathy and toleration for each other; we should gladly bear one another's burdens and so fulfill the law of Christ. Heaven ordains to each a particular suffering that "connects the family of man into one household" (1:2.12.144–45). Dale believes that the feeling of sympathy distinguishes humans from the brutes. Man, he says, must experience sorrow and joy not in himself alone, but in the joy and sorrow of those around him. For "he who feels only for himself abjures his very nature as man; for do we not say of one who has no tenderness for mankind that he is inhuman; and do we not call him who sorrows with the sorrowful humane?" (1:2.12.145).

Randal Leslie symbolizes intellect corrupted by ambition. His ruling beliefs are that knowledge is power and that success in life justifies all things—the reverse of Lenny's love of knowledge for its own sake. Representing intellectual evil, Randal's errors arise from his head outrunning his heart. Circumstance and poor home training also act to defeat him, as he takes no nutriment from the values of the heart and learns no useful moral lessons at home.

Audley Egerton, who exemplifies the ideal of the practical, represents Bulwer's model politician. Whatever success he achieves in the Commons arises from his reputation as a true gentleman. The epitomy of reserve, dignity, and self-control, he is admired by all as a thoughtful, weighty speaker in the Commons. He is a moderate in politics, often acting independent of party. As to his character, Bulwer's narrator claims that his courage, energetic will, and regal liberality contrast with his simplicity in personal tastes and habits. All these attributes serve "to invest the practical man with those spells which are usually confined to the Ideal one. But, indeed, Audley Egerton was an Ideal,—the Ideal of the Practical. Not the mere vulgar, plodding, red-tape machine of petty business, but the man of strong sense, inspired by inflexible energy and guided to definite earthly objects" (1:7.19.160). Yet such qualities do not endear him to Randal, who hates him because he has not reduced his mentor to a mere tool or stepping stone. Randal rightly fears that Egerton can see through him and accurately read his corrupt heart. To his friend, Harley L'Estrange, Egerton says that in Randal he finds the ambitious soul, eye, and step of the Jesuit. Randal dislikes his patron because he has warned him to expect nothing from him in his will.

My Novel proved the most popular of the Caxton novels, and with good reason, as it is Bulwer's best domestic novel. Its overall plan to unite the feuding social factions in England—the economic liberals and all those who opposed their heartless doctrines of profit at the expense of human sympathy—required a panoramic design filled with characters from all the social classes. Bulwer succeeded admirably in this task, adeptly balancing the demands of multiple plotting with superbly drawn portraits of people from all walks of life. His Americanized vulgarian, Dick Avenel, his high-souled conservative politicians, his rural squire and parson, and Lenny Fairfield are finely drawn characters who not only exemplify many different classes and types, but also manage to come alive as individuals.

In *My Novel* there is also a fuller and more detailed picture of the House of Commons and English political life at the start of the nineteenth-century than in any of Bulwer's other novels. The election scenes and the political mini-history of the Tory party's dissolution are impressive pieces of political reportage, nearly the equal of Trollope's political novels in accuracy and dramatic color. In addition, Bulwer managed effectively to espouse his metaphysical thesis about the ideal, the true, the real, and the beautiful.

What Will He Do with It? as an Illustration of False Pride and Noble Self-Sacrifice

The popularity of *My Novel* led Bulwer to try to recapture its success with *What Will He Do with It?*, the final novel in his Caxton series on contemporary life. He began work on it in January 1857 and completed the manuscript in early February 1858, the same month that he joined Lord Derby's government as colonial secretary. By the spring of 1857, Bulwer had written enough of the novel that he could send John Forster several opening chapters for his comments. On 27 April 1857, Forster wrote back enthusiastically that he "hugely liked" the book's initial chapters, a view Robert Louis Stevenson seconded years later in describing books that influenced his own writing.[31] Forster particularly praised Bulwer's portrait of the crippled strolling player, William Waife, a character he thought "something new" and capable of "infinite growth" as the story progressed.[32] In May the same year, he told Bulwer that he had "done nothing finer, nothing fuller of subtle touches of genius and wisdom and humanity, than {Guy} Darrell and his surroundings."[33] John Blackwood, who continued to advise Bulwer in literary matters, suggested some of the character traits that Bulwer gave to Waife, Jasper Losely, and Arabella Crane. Dickens supplied the book with its title, praising its author for "the constructive art displayed throughout the whole story."[34]

What Will He Do with It? was serialized in *Blackwood's Magazine* in twenty monthly installments from June 1857 to January 1859. Early in 1859, Blackwood brought it out in a hefty four-volume book edition totaling 1,414 pages. For both the serial and the book rights, Blackwood paid Bulwer £3,000, more than double the sum he received for *The Caxtons* in 1849. Such lucrative earnings allowed Bulwer the luxury of writing less frequently, and for the first time in his writing career he felt financially secure. And well he might, for in 1853 the publisher George Routledge gave Bulwer £20,000 for a ten-year option to reprint nineteen of his most popular novels in an inexpensive edition.

Unlike its two predecessors in the series, *What Will He Do with It?* has few analogues with the eighteenth-century novel. Gone are the narrative proems of Fielding and the structural whimsicalities of Sterne, though there is one Sterne-like chapter. Titled "Dénouement," it contains a single word: "Poodles!"[35] Instead, Bulwer's novel takes its formal design from the Victorian novel, especially from Dickens, whose influence Ernest A. Baker saw all through the book. Waife and his granddaughter Sophy seem "a loan from *The Old Curiosity Shop*" (1841),[36] and the other characters can be divided into Dickensian comic grotesques and criminals. In form, Bulwer's novel may best be classified as a romance of real life, a term appearing with increasing frequency on the title page of novels published after 1820. Such novels featured romance, crime, and the improbable, all made probable and immediate by realistic narratives and contemporary settings. Along with the romance of real life, Bulwer's novel contains recognizable ingredients from the stage melodrama. It employs nearly equal portions of comedy, sentiment, villainy, and mystery, illustrating the truth of the old theatrical maxim:

Make them laugh, make them cry, but above all else make them wait (for the mystery's solution).

The novel's title refers to the book's intricate multiple plotting, the constructive art that Dickens so admired. As Bulwer's grandson noted, *What Will He Do with It?* features some fourteen different characters "all of which are intimately connected with the story, all separate links in one chain, each one having an influence at some moment on [the lives or] fortunes of all the others."[37] At the novel's start they are scattered in both time and place, and the question that arises in the reader's mind as each character is introduced is, What will the author do with them?[38]

Despite its secrets and mysteries, the book is not a sensation novel. Bulwer's aim is not to thrill, shock, or awe his reader, but to forcefully elaborate his ruling theme about self-sacrifice. Some of the novel's characters are ennobled by their self-abnegation (William Waife and Arabella Crane) because it arises from virtue; others (Guy Darrell and Lady Caroline Montfort) fail to lead happy, useful, or successful lives because their pride commands them to sacrifice themselves needlessly to some ideal of honor, duty, dignity, or reputation. Such self-immolation, Bulwer argues, prevents its devotees from facing necessary truths to free themselves of blinding pride.

In his novel, Bulwer focuses on the sacrificial obstinancy of two of the best-hearted men (Guy Darrell and William Waife), showing how Darrell, in his pointless self-sacrifice, offers up the joys of his youth to a false idol of pride and name only to blight his happiness and ruin his career. In contrast, Waife, as an act of virtue, delivers up the comforts of his old age to assume the blame for his son's crime, mutely appealing to heaven for eventual vindication. His long suffering heals him of his early shiftless character, and over the years he is ennobled by his self-denial and fortitude. Both men illustrate Bulwer's belief that sympathy and experience are the true ways to read the human heart.

What Will He Do with It? is inferior in quality to its two predecessors in the Caxton series. Despite its contrasting themes and artful plots, it reflects Bulwer's growing weariness with the realistic mode. While the novel clearly illustrates both the nobility and the needlessness of self-sacrifice, Bulwer fails to achieve fully realized characters. Most of them do not transcend their assigned typifications to become individual beings for whom the reader really cares.

Gentleman Waife is an unpleasing example of the bathetic and thus more suitable for the boards of a Victorian melodrama—the "pathetic old man" stereotype. The other leading character, Guy Darrell, represents a role Bulwer had drawn more effectively before in Ernest Maltravers and Harley L'Estrange. Some thirty years after Byron's death, Bulwer's continued use of Byronic heroes becomes an indulgence that is neither novel nor interesting.

Yet despite the failure of his last Caxton novel, Bulwer made significant contributions to the novel of domestic realism, for his comic doctrines of conciliation and cordiality pointed to Meredith's comic theories. Bulwer's political scenes were the best-informed analyses of English political life before Trollope's Palliser novels. While Bulwer produced nothing to equal Thackeray and George Eliot's novels of domestic life, his *The Caxtons* and *My Novel* may be read today with genuine pleasure. *What Will He Do with It?* was the last domestic novel Bulwer wrote; following it he returned to the metaphysical mode for the remainder of his writing career.

Chapter Seven
Occult and Scientific Romances

Writing in 1913, Bulwer's grandson felt compelled to set the record straight about his grandfather's attitudes on the occult and about his public reputation arising from such arcane interests. He refuted the belief Bulwer only wrote about the occult to increase the sale of his books or to exploit the public's appetite for sensationalism.[1] Nor, he claimed, was Bulwer's knowledge of the occult cursory. He "did not study magic for the sake of writing about it; still less did he write about it, without having studied it."[2] Bulwer's examination of occult subjects was serious, discriminating, and extensive.[3]

But he had no illusions regarding psychical phenomena. He carefully scrutinized spirit rappings, clairvoyance, and mesmerism and "found them all disappointingly unconvincing and unprofitable."[4] Bulwer's beliefs, his grandson claimed, conformed exactly to those held by "members of the Psychical Research Society of the present day—anxious to learn something that would extend the horizon of human knowledge and experience, yet forced to confess that nothing . . . he had witnessed himself really justified any definite conclusions."[5] Lastly, Victor Lytton wished to lay to rest wild stories about Bulwer's imagined possession of occult powers. One story in particular he disavowed—the much repeated account of Bulwer passing through a room at Knebworth, believing himself to be invisible, and reappearing later in the day to greet his guests as if meeting them for the first time.[6] Such stories, Lytton complained, made good copy, but really stemmed from more prosaic causes. If Bulwer failed to notice a guest, it was because of his shyness, reverie, or literary preoccupations.[7]

Robert Lee Wolff, who has written extensively on Bulwer and the occult, rejects this official family version of Bulwer as inaccurate and misleading. Bulwer's views on the occult were more complex than Victor Lytton suggests in describing his grandfather as the equivalent of the disinterested modern psychic researcher. Wolff believes Bulwer was ambivalent about the occult. He enjoyed the public reputation of being thought a sorcerer while protesting that there was probably nothing to the occult—no demonstrable proof of its existence as scientific fact.[8] Bulwer loved mystification as much as he liked mysticism. He especially relished the notoriety of being a member of the revived Rosicrucian order in which he rose to the high office of grand patron sometime in the early 1850s.

Modern Bulwerian studies have established two facts: for nearly forty years Bulwer sustained a fascination for all things occult, and he assiduously read most of the classic texts written about the occult. His knowledge in this field was both comprehensive and profound. He knew all the Neoplatonist writings, particularly those by Iamblichus and Proclus.[9] Bulwer also read the eleventh-century Byzantine writer Michael Psellus, who wrote learned treatises on demons. And he was familiar with the studies of Paracelsus, Heinrich Cornelius Agrippa, and Jean Baptiste Van Helmont, all major writers on alchemy. At the same time he kept current on the latest developments in physiology, philosophy, and psychology, subjects allied to his interest in the occult. Like other prominent Victorian men of letters, Bulwer attentively followed the latest findings in psychical research. He attended public demonstrations that explored the efficacy of phrenology, mesmerism, and spiritualism. With Dickens and Thackeray, Bulwer supported the psychical research undertaken by Dr. John Elliotson and Dr. John Ashburner, the two most respected figures in early Victorian psychic studies. He also patronized spiritualists and magicians like Daniel Dunglas Home and Éliphas Lévi, whose activities were suspect to many because of their lack of scientific objectivity. Bulwer experimented in private, examining for himself the merits of mesmerism and spiritualism. His letters to friends sympathetic to psychical research documented the frequency of séances held at his country estate at Knebworth. In collaboration with Home, Bulwer kept systematic records of these sessions, describing in some detail their proceedings.

Zicci and *Zanoni* as Occult Parables Reaffirming the Christian Virtues of Faith, Love, and Self-Sacrifice

The earliest sources among Bulwer's writings for both *Zicci* and *Zanoni* date back to 1825 and the period of his apprenticeship to fiction. At that time he experimented with mystical subjects in an unpublished fragment about the Rosicrucian Brotherhood. In it Bulwer introduces several themes—the quest for superhuman wisdom and the ability to prolong life—that he later developed more fully in *Zanoni*.

His grandson claimed that the controlling ideas for *Zanoni* could be traced back to 1835, when Bulwer first began his research into the occult sciences. With his mind occupied by such esoteric themes, the character of Mejnour and the main outlines of *Zanoni* came to him in a dream.[10] Few details of this dream survived except that it dealt with a sage who extended his life over several centuries by imbibing an elixir of life compounded from herbs. In 1838 Bulwer published a version of his dream in a fragmentary novella called *Zicci* in William Harrison Ainsworth's magazine, the *Monthly Chronicle*. *Zicci*, offers essentially the same themes later found in *Zanoni* (1842)—the ninety-page *Zicci* fragment appears in expanded form in books 2 and 3 of *Zanoni*.

In *Zicci* Bulwer presents a secret brotherhood of immortalists who possess superhuman knowledge, predict the future, read the thoughts of others, disappear in a cloud of smoke, and seek recruits to replenish their dwindling order and to rule the world. At the story's center is a mysterious preternatural hero (Zicci) who sacrifices his marvelous powers in exchange for the love of a woman (the actress Isabel di Pisani), and a foolish, impetuous artist (Clarence Glyndon) who willingly surrenders human love to become a neophyte in the brotherhood. The fragment ends as Glyndon becomes the postulant of Mejnour (one of the brotherhood) and as both retire to a mountain castle to begin Glyndon's novitiate. These rudimentary themes are given their fullest expression in *Zanoni*, Bulwer's final version of the story.

Saunders and Otley published *Zanoni* in early February 1842 in three volumes. From its first appearance, Bulwer feared the public's reaction to the book, certain its lofty moral would puzzle reader and critic alike. Anticipating such a response, he slyly affixed an epigraph to the title page of volume one that read, "I cannot make head nor tail on't."[11] *Zanoni*, Bulwer predicted to John Forster in their correspondence, "will be no favorite with that largest of all asses—the English Public" because it "shoots too much over the heads of the people to hit the popular taste."[12] But he also told Forster the novel provided him with an opportunity to symbolize and typify his ideas in fictional form.

While the first edition had no dedication, Bulwer supplied one for the 1845 printing, inscribing *Zanoni* to the sculptor John Gibson, whom he first met in Rome in 1833. In his dedicatory epistle, Bulwer said that Gibson's art illustrated the principle he wished to convey in *Zanoni:* that the artist must not work in isolation from society. Yet the attributes he praised in Gibson's life only blurred this aim. Gibson, he said, was remarkable for having escaped the worst perils besetting artists—"the debasing tendencies of Commerce, and the angry rivalries of Competition" (v).

Bulwer saw a parallel in their careers. Both had been superficially judged by the public, both had refused to lower their tastes to please current fashions in art, and both took delight in conceiving and performing their art despite public misunderstanding and critical hostility. In their retreat from "Agora to the Cave" (from the public to the private artistic voice), they shared a common bond of artistic sympathy that united them in "the Everlasting Brotherhood [of artists], of whose being *Zanoni* is the type" (vi). Bulwer's dedication reflected both his own harsh treatment by critics and his desire to retire from the realistic (Agora) to the metaphysical (cave) writing mode. But more importantly, the dedicatory epistle was intended as self-praise, for Bulwer felt that the "simplicity, calm, and concentration" found in Gibson's sculpture were present in his own fiction too (vi).

With the preface to the 1853 edition, Bulwer printed Harriet Martineau's key to both the characters and *Zanoni*'s central argument, which thereafter appeared in all editions of the novel. The function, he claimed, of the 1853 preface and concluding note was to clarify his artistic aims for *Zanoni*. Robert Lee Wolff, however, speaks for most modern readers in finding Bulwer's preface "disingenuous, defensive, and rather adding to the mystification . . . that elucidating it."[13] This confusion arose from Bulwer's refusal to say how far Miss Martineau's interpretation represented his own intentions. He claimed her solution was but one of many possible for the novel. Clearly Bulwer enjoyed the interest taken in his book, and in the preface he sought to increase his readers' curiosity, not diminish it by providing further explications of *Zanoni*'s subtleties. Miss Martineau's key, Bulwer remarked, showed the interest excited among the novel's readers, who liked to dive into the more abstruse meanings beneath the surface of his narrative.

Bulwer felt compelled, however, to add a few words, not in explanation of *Zanoni*'s mysteries, but upon the principles that permitted them. He stressed that *Zanoni* was not an allegory, as some of his readers supposed, but rather a novel based on typical meanings. Unlike allegories, which were personations of "distinct and definite things" (virtues or qualities), typical meanings were but "moral suggestions, more or less numerous, more or less subtle" (421–22). Bulwer believed a writer who conveyed typical meanings "may express them in myriads," but need not "disentangle all [their] hues [of meaning] . . . into the light he seeks to cast upon truth . . . [for] great masters . . . wisely leave . . . each mind to guess at such truths as best please and instruct it" (421–22). In *Zanoni* Bulwer treated "our positive life" as seen "through a spiritual medium" (vii). The novel's design, he claimed, was analogous to his epic poem, *King Arthur* (1848), because both featured a fine balance "between the external events which are all that the superficial behold on the surface of human affairs, and the subtle and intellectual agencies which . . . influence the conduct of individuals, and shape . . . the destinies of the World" (vii).

Zanoni differs in design and theme from most of Bulwer's earlier novels because in it he is concerned less with plot than with the delineation of types, characters, and themes unique in fiction. His novel is best read as a fairy tale written for adults, a kind of metaphysical parable of first moral causes. Panoramic in scope and complex in character groupings, *Zanoni* is a composite novel shaped by five complementary controlling patterns. It is an occult parable reaffirming the Christian virtues of faith, love and self-sacrifice; a spiritual autobiography and bildungsroman tracing Clarence Glyndon's rites of passage to personal and moral maturity; a political polemic against the ideas causing and carrying forward the French Revolution; a treatise on romantic aesthetics debating the efficacy of feeling over reason and the ideal over the actual in art; and a discourse on the natural causes underlying the occult sciences, reflecting Bulwer's belief that the supernatural is but the natural as yet undiscovered.

Such a seemingly cacophonous composition is harmonized through its unity in theme and supporting design. Robert Lee Wolff notes that *Zanoni*'s design follows the four stages of divinely inspired enthusiasms found in Plato's *Phaedrus,* which Bulwer knew through Thomas Taylor's recent translation of Hermias's *On the Mysteries*

(1820).[14] Hermias identifies Plato's four stages of enthusiasm as the musical, the mystical, the prophetic, and the amatory. Each stage organizes at least one of Bulwer's major themes in *Zanoni*. Musical enthusiasm shapes the story of visionary composer-violinist Gaetano Pisani and his singer daughter, Viola (book 1, *The Musician*). Mystical enthusiasm inspires the occult apprenticeship of Clarence Glyndon (books 2, *Art, Love, and Wonder;* 3, *Theurgia;* 4, *The Dweller of the Threshold;* and 5, *The Effects of the Elixir*). Prophetic enthusiasm fuels Bulwer's conservative political attack against the horrors of the French Revolution (book 7, *The Reign of Terror*). And amatory enthusiasm dramatizes Zanoni's discovery that only through self-sacrifice and death can he discover love, true happiness, and eternal life (book 8).

Bulwer unites these thematic strands—the epistemological, the occult, the political, the aesthetic, and the religious— by showing how they are interconnected. His controlling thesis in *Zanoni* is that political visionaries like Robespierre and quixotic students like Glyndon fail to attain either reform or supreme wisdom because they attempt what is beyond their power. Glyndon's eagerness to learn, because of his refusal to wait and acquire knowledge slowly through proper preparation at each phase of his ordeal, only produces a hideous demon (the Dweller of the Threshold) who persecutes and punishes him for his impetuosity and intellectual presumption.[15] Robespierre and the other French political theorists parallel Glyndon's failure. Their haste in erecting a political utopia based on freedom and equality is doomed from the start because they refuse to progress by gradual reforms. In their impatience to speed up political and social change, they turn to violence (the equivalent of Glyndon's heady elixir) and bring upon themselves and France a horrible demon (the Reign of Terror) that punishes them for their lawlessness and reliance on bloodshed. Bulwer postulates that had the reformers moved more slowly and kept within the law, they might have achieved true freedom for France. But what is in every human being's power—exemplified by Zanoni's sacrificial death to save Viola's life—is the capacity to triumph over fear and death through love (love dares all, Bulwer claims) and to achieve in death the promise of eternal life.

This spiritual achievement complements Bulwer's aesthetic argument that the loftiest order of art is that in which one struggles upward to approach God. Only in the ideal school of art can we raise ourselves from the actual and the real to the great and the beautiful. In conduct, as in art, there is an ideal based on grandeur of thought and beauty of conception by which we should exalt the real and the actual. Bulwer links art to religion when Glyndon breaks free of his dread specter and learns from Zanoni that without religious faith there can be no notion of excellence. For the ideal in art is synonymous with religious faith: both prize something wiser, happier, and diviner than can be seen on earth. And in Bulwer's own art—one aspiring to approach God in its message through ascending stages of Platonic enthusiasms—he seeks to show his readers what they cannot see by themselves—that, as Mejnour and Zanoni discover, to live forever upon this earth is but to live in ourselves. Only through love, selfless action, and faith can we hope to achieve something more divine.

The narrative frame introducing *Zanoni* provides a key to the novel's controlling thesis and design, traces the origin of *Zicci* and *Zanoni* to published works, and supplies hints for the way Bulwer wanted his novel interpreted. In this introduction the novel's anonymous editor describes how he came to possess the manuscripts he eventually publishes as *Zicci* and *Zanoni*. Searching for material about the Rosicrucians, the editor visits a London occult bookshop located near Covent Garden. There he meets an elderly painter with singular habits and eccentric opinions. The painter proves to be Clarence Glyndon, now matured in character and at the end of his long spiritual pilgrimage. His youthful thirst for occult knowledge has been replaced by a devout belief in Christianity. He occupies his time chiefly in acts of quiet and unostentatious goodness, carrying out the charitable duties of a good Samaritan. The two men become friends, and over the years they frequently discuss art, politics, and the occult sciences. Eventually, Glyndon dies, leaving the editor both a handsome bequest and a 940-page manuscript written in an odd code. The editor spends several years deciphering Glyndon's hieroglyphics before translating enough to publish a fragment *(Zicci)* in a periodical. This fragment excites enough public interest to encourage the editor to continue translating. At this point, he discovers Glyndon made two copies of his manuscript, one longer and more elaborate than the other. The editor translates and publishes the longer version in 1842 as the three-volume novel.

Zanoni, the editor claims, is and is not a romance. It contains "truth for those who can comprehend it," but it becomes "an extravagance for those who cannot" (xviii). He confesses that the novel's poetical conception and design—its four-part Platonic division—caused him to insert several interpolations of his own to clarify its obscure passages. Whatever pleases the reader in *Zanoni* arises from the editor's work, and whatever is displeasing must be blamed on Glyndon.

In Glyndon's conversations with the editor, Bulwer furnishes directions for rightly reading the novel. About the Rosicrucians, for example, Glyndon claims that while they are respectable, virtuous, severe in moral precept, and ardent in Christian faith, they form but one branch of the occult fraternity. Others—the Chaldeans, Gymnosophists, and Platonists—possess more transcendent powers and claim more illustrious origins. Through Glyndon, Bulwer reminds the reader that both Zanoni's and Mejnour's remarkable powers derive from a far older occult tradition than the Rosicrucians. In fact, *Zanoni* should not be read as a Rosicrucian romance but as an occult parable based on Chaldean and Platonist concepts.

In another area—Glyndon's views on the first French Revolution—Bulwer's motivation for including revolutionary scenes in *Zanoni* can be seen. The editor notes that unlike many who write about the French Revolution, Glyndon lived through it as an eyewitness. He speaks not as a student who only reads and reasons on the subject, but as someone who has personally suffered in the revolution. As a consequence, Glyndon cannot regard the "crimes" of that period with the "philosophical leniency" of enlightened writers who gloss over "the massacres of the past" (xv). As this passage makes clear, Bulwer seeks to attack liberal apologists who justify Robespierre's crimes as the inevitable result of revolutionary progress. Bulwer's conservative political thesis in *Zanoni* is identical to the argument in his prose essay "The Reign of Terror," printed in the *Foreign Quarterly Review* (July 1842).[16]

The introduction to *Zanoni* also alerts readers to Bulwer's aesthetic argument. Glyndon tells the editor that all the arts are connected, as are the sciences. In art and literature a distinction needs to be made between the real and the true—between "the imitation of actual life and the exaltation of Nature into the Ideal" (xiii). The first represents the Dutch school, the other the Greek. Today, Glyndon notes, the Dutch (the real) rules supreme—"our . . . poets are all for simplicity and Betty Foy" (xiii). Critics, he claims, "hold it the highest praise of a work of imagination to say that its characters are exact to common life" (xiii). They see Shakespeare as a realist, while in Glyndon (and Bulwer's) view, Shakespeare never once drew "a character to be met with in actual life," nor once "descended to a passion that is false or a personage who is real" (xiii). Bulwer places Shakespeare among the ideal school as one who typifies his characters and seeks universal truths. Most importantly, Bulwer wishes to locate *Zanoni* in the idealist school as a work that follows Shakespeare's lead in its artistic conception and execution.

Public response to *Zanoni* proved mixed. Thomas Carlyle, who previously thought Bulwer but a "poor fribble" of a writer, believed *Zanoni* would be a "liberating voice for much that lay dumb imprisoned in human souls"; it would "shake old deep-set errors looser in their rootings, and thro' such chinks . . . let in light on dark places . . . in need of light."[17] Anne Thackeray, the novelist's daughter, felt that "Zanoni and the catlike spirit of the threshold [were] as vivid . . . as any of the people who [came] to dinner."[18]

Some of the periodical critics, as Bulwer predicted, dismissed the book as incomprehensible. Bulwer, the *Athenaeum*'s critic complained, deprived his characters of any sense of reality by following the ideal mode in the novel. Even in a philosophical extravaganza like *Zanoni,* there must be "coherence, adjustment of parts, climax of interest . . . if it [is] to [be ranked] as a work of art."[19] In his view, *Zanoni* was but a strange patchwork of things discordant. Both *Zicci* and *Zanoni* featured only "tinselled truisms [figuring] as new discoveries, and obscurity of meaning [passing] for elevation of thought."[20]

In contrast, the reviewer for the *Literary Gazette* greatly admired *Zanoni,* thinking it "wild, [but] true."[21] To him, Bulwer's novel possessed "rather more of poetry than of prose."[22] It had fine imagination and was "neither a novel nor a romance; but a creation of genius, combining things possible and impossible, credible and incredible, the body and the soul, the realities and the dreams of life—in itself a dazzling dream."[23] In a word, he felt *Zanoni* "an effusion of genius."[24] The *Examiner* reviewer believed *Zanoni* "less designed to amuse than to set its readers thinking"; it was "eloquent and thoughtful . . . full of Platonism of all sorts."[25] *Zanoni,* he continued, contained "richness of thought" and much "deep feeling."[26] He praised its supernatural passages for avoiding the commonplace vulgarity of terror so common in the Radcliffe school of writers.

Writing to John Forster, Bulwer admitted *Zanoni* would never be seen by the public with the author's eye, but for himself he declared the book "wonderful if read in the proper spirit."[27] Modern critics rank *Zanoni* as one of Bulwer's great masterpieces, correctly seeing it as a romance rather than a realistic novel. Some, like Jack Lindsay, view *Zanoni* as a source for Sidney Carton's noble self-sacrifice in Dickens's *A Tale of Two Cities* (1859). And Joseph Fradin identifies Bulwer as a major connection between the "Romantic believers in the energy of the Imagination and . . . symbolist and surrealist" writers of a later generation.[28]

"The Haunted and the Haunters" as a Dramatization of Bulwer's Theory of Magic

"The Haunted and the Haunters"—Bulwer's story about a night spent in a haunted house—first appeared in *Blackwood's Edinburgh Magazine* in August 1859. After its publication, Bulwer revised it since it duplicated parts of his next novel, *A Strange Story* (1861–62). The second (shorter) version, the one always reprinted after 1861, he reissued in *Tales from Blackwood's* (1st ser., vol. 10, 1858–61). T. H. S. Escott thought the story "startlingly suggestive and creepily enthralling," a judgment upheld by its frequent reprinting in modern anthologies of supernatural fiction.[29] There is strong evidence Bulwer based part of his popular short story on the séances Daniel Dunglas Home conducted at Knebworth during the mid-1850s. In a book published in 1890, Homes's widow claimed:

Half the phenomena described by [the story's] solitary watcher in the haunted house—the luminous form collapsing gradually into a vivid globule, the loud measured knocks at the bedhead, the vibrations of the floor, the grasp of an unseen hand, the hand emerging from under the table to seize the letters on it, the multitude of fiery sparks that flitted through the darkness—read like a transcript of Lord Lytton's records of his séances with Home at Knebworth. . . . The material phenomena of those séances have never been more graphically and powerfully described than in The Haunted and the Haunters.[30]

Bulwer's thriller does indeed reproduce these phenomena, and, as does *Zanoni,* argues that "the Supernatural is the Impossible, and that what is called supernatural is only a something in the laws of nature of which we have hitherto been ignorant."[31] The story's thesis is the closest Bulwer ever came to publicly declaring his belief in magic, the term he applied to phenomena beyond scientific explanation.

Set in contemporary London, "The Haunted and the Haunters" belongs to the destructive ghost story subgenre—a formula in which a person must face and exorcise a malignant force. The story's unnamed narrator enters a house in Oxford Street reputed to be haunted day and night. None of the lodgers who have rented the house stay more than three days, and no two describe exactly the same phenomena. Accompanied by his servant F—— and a bull terrier, the narrator equips himself with only a pistol, dagger, matches, and a volume of Lord Macaulay's essays. Inside, he immediately encounters strange phenomena—footsteps and whispering voices, chairs moving by themselves, an unseen child's footprints on the floor, doors suddenly shutting and locking, and venomous exhalations rising from chinks in the floor.

The narrator pauses in his tale to theorize and to articulate the story's thesis about the impossibility of the supernatural. His own theory is that the supernatural does not exist, and what the world calls supernatural is merely something unexplainable in the laws of nature. In all the wonders the present age records as facts, some "material living agency is always required" (312). All such marvels—spirit manifestations, odd sounds, automatic writing, levitation, and spirit ectoplasms—supposing no imposture, must have "a human being like ourselves by whom, or through whom, the effects presented to human beings are produced" (312). This is true, he claims, of the "now familiar phenomena of mesmerism or electrobiology," for "the mind of the person operated on is affected through a material living agent" (312). All he has witnessed so far in the house in Oxford Street must originate in some human being "gifted by constitution with the power" to create such remarkable events (313). The narrator ends his aside to the reader priding himself that his theory is more philosophical than superstitious.

This philosophy enables the narrator to remain tranquil in temper, but his tranquility is immediately tested by a second, more horrifying series of apparitions. He becomes aware of a darkness shaping itself into a human form of gigantic dimensions with two malignant, serpent eyes looking down at him. Multicolored bubbles appear, and from them, as from the shell of an egg, monstrous things burst forth into the room—larvae so bloodless and hideous that they

cannot be described. By focusing his stubborn will against the sha-
dow, the narrator overcomes its intense evil. When lights reappear
from the candles and the grate, the narrator discovers his dog lying
in the corner of the room with its neck broken. Nothing else happens
during the rest of the night, but before leaving the house, the
narrator revisits the room where he had been imprisoned. He believes
this room is the source of all the mechanisms of the phenomena.

The narrator resolves to clear up all the mysteries associated with
the house in Oxford Street. His theories on magic reflect Bulwer's.
Refusing to attribute the mysteries to imposture, the narrator prefers
to believe the house contains some power akin to mesmerism but
far superior to it. To prove his theory, the narrator convinces
J——, the owner of the haunted house, to open the walls and
remove the floor of the room believed to be the source of all the
manifestations. Once this is done, they discover a secret room below
the haunted room containing an iron safe fixed to the wall. Inside
the safe they find a number of occult instruments—bottles of col-
orless liquids, glass tubes, lumps of rock crystal and amber, an iron
rod, and a lodestone of great power. Also found is a curious minature
portrait of a middle-aged man with a hideous serpentlike face.
Engraved on the back of the minature is a pentacle with a ladder;
the third step of the ladder has the date 1765 on it. Following the
inscription is a name the narrator recognizes as belonging to a
charlatan who made a great sensation in London years earlier before
fleeing the country to escape the charge of murdering his mistress
and rival. They also find a small, thin book placed upon a saucer
of crystal filled with a clear liquid. A compass floats on the liquid
with its needle shifting rapidly around the dial face. As the narrator
removes the saucer from its hazel drawer, he feels a strong electrical
shock throughout his body. The walls of the room shake as the
contents of the broken saucer spill on the floor. He opens the book
and discovers it contains a single sheet of vellum, on which is written
in old Latin: "On all that it can reach within these walls—sentient
or inanimate, living or dead—as moves the needle, so work my
will! Accursed be the house, and restless be the dwellers therein"
(327). Finding nothing else, they burn the book and its anathema.
Later the owner razes the foundations of the side of the house supporting the secret room. These alterations exorcise the evil magi-
cian's influence in the house forever.

A Strange Story as the Spiritual Reeducation of a Materialist

With his return to the metaphysical mode in "The Haunted and the Haunters" (1859) and *A Strange Story* (1861–62), Bulwer began his last artistic phase. Like *Zanoni*, *A Strange Story*'s ruling idea originated from a dream, one Bulwer's son claimed to be even more interesting than the novel later founded upon it.[32] Bulwer completed *Story* at the end of 1860 and gladly accepted Dickens's offer to serialize it in his magazine, *All the Year Round*. On 4 December 1860, Bulwer concluded the financial details with Dickens, agreeing to accept £1,500 for the novel, £1,200 for its transfer to book publication, and an additional £300 for American serial rights.[33] *A Strange Story* appeared anonymously in *All the Year Round*, running in weekly numbers from 10 August 1861 to 8 March 1862. Sampson and Low printed the two-volume book edition in 1862.

Twelve days before *Story* began its run in *All the Year Round*, Bulwer wrote John Forster and expressed his fears about the public reception of his new novel. While *Story* was "original and a psychological curiosity," he felt unsure of "its effects either with the few or the many."[34] The Forster letter initiated a complicated round of correspondence between Bulwer and Dickens about the necessity of adding a preface to the novel, or providing a key (like Harriet Martineau's for *Zanoni*), or placing more interpretive explanations in the Faber-Fenwick conversations to make clear his artistic aims. Bulwer worried his readers would not understand that the novel's occult scenes—particularly the closing one—contained the book's symbolic meaning and explained its controlling philosophy. Dickens, acting as both editor and friend, managed the skittish author magnificently, sympathizing, consoling, and calming Bulwer. Above all, he gave Bulwer sound literary advice. Dickens told him every story should contain in itself all that is essential to its own explanation. Prefaces, he warned, cause more trouble than they resolve. Recognizing the good sense in Dickens's admonitions, Bulwer allowed *Story* to appear in *All the Year Round* without any additional interpretative aids. But early, unfavorable notices from the critics led Bulwer to write a short preface for the two-volume book edition, one that would explain *Story*'s interior meanings and artistic aims.

In this preface Bulwer claimed that the thinking of Pierre Maine de Biran (1766–1824) represented the changes in European thought since the close of the eighteenth century. Maine de Biran began his career as a disciple of Etienne Bonnot de Condillac's doctrine of materialism. Observing certain phenomena inexplicable to the senses alone, he added a second stage of human life beyond Condillac's, one that embraced the concept of free will and self-consciousness, uniting matter with mind. Yet Maine de Biran felt something further was needed, some key to the marvels that neither matter nor mind sufficed to explain. He proposed a third life of man, which he identified as the soul. Thus in man there were three "orders of faculties" ideally "in accord and in harmony" with each other.[35] Through the agencies of romance (the supernatural), Bulwer sought to conduct his "bewildered hero [Allen Fenwick] towards the same goal [belief in the soul] to which Philosophy leads its luminous Student [Maine de Biran]" (vi). Fenwick's goal, paralleling Maine de Biran's intellectual growth, was to transcend body and mind to the life of the spirit, recognizing that "Christianity alone embraces the whole Man" (vi). In Fenwick's spiritual reeducation Bulwer attempted to refute Darwin's theory of evolution—the *Origin of Species* had appeared three years earlier in 1859—by employing science (Maine de Biran and others cited in the novel's footnotes) to document the existence of the human soul and to bolster Christianity's moral authority.

Bulwer's preface also provided explanations for *Story*'s symbolic meanings. Through the "haze of romance," Bulwer said, the reader should detect certain images informing the book's philosophy. They were, first

the image of sensuous, soulless Nature [Margrave], such as the Materialist had conceived it; secondly, the image of Intellect [Fenwick], obstinately separating all its inquiries from the belief in the spiritual essence and destiny of man, and incurring all kinds of perplexity and resorting to all kinds of visionary speculation before it settles at last into the simple faith which unites the philosopher and the infant; and thirdly, the image of the erring but pure-thoughted visionary [Lilian Ashleigh], seeking overmuch on this earth to separate soul from mind, till innocence itself is led astray by a phantom, and reason is lost in the space between earth and the stars (ix).

In a letter to Dickens, Bulwer elaborated further on these characters as types. Margrave, he claimed, represented "the sensuous material principle of Nature" and Ayesha, his mistress "with her black veil, unknown song, and her skeleton attendant, Death, is Nature as a materialist, like Fenwick, sees her."[36] Fenwick, Bulwer claimed, "is the type of the intellect that divorces itself from the spiritual, and disdaining to acknowledge the first cause [belief in God], and the beliefs that spring from it, is cheated by the senses themselves, and falls into all kinds of visionary mistakes and illusions [materialism and skepticism] similar to those of great reasoners, like Hume, La Place, and La March."[37] Lilian, he noted, exemplified soul divorced from the intellect, indulging in "mystic ecstacies which end in the loss of [her] reason."[38] Each character "has need of the other, and their union is really brought thro' the heart— Fenwick recognizing soul and God, thro' love and sorrow" and Lilian struggling "back to reason and life, thro' her love and her desire to live for the belov'd one's sake."[39] Bulwer identified Mrs. Colonel Margaret Poyntz as symbolizing the polite world.

In his preface Bulwer remarked that he employed the supernatural to convey his novel's philosophical thesis, for only "in fairy fiction drest . . . [does] Romance [give] admission to truths severe" (vii). He justified its inclusion, as in the past, by stressing its legitimacy in ancient epics and prose romances. Art, he argued, cannot "express either Man or Nature" because "Man is not man, nor Nature, nature . . . without some gleams of the supernatural" (vii–viii).

Yet *Story* had another artistic aim, one whose truth Bulwer felt too severe for public discussion in his preface. He described this aim to John Forster in a letter written on 3 December 1861. In regard to the supernatural he told Forster, "What I really wish to imply is this—without taking up mesmerism and spirit manifestation. I want to intimate that in their recorded marvels which are attested by hundreds and believed by many thousands, things yet more incredible than those which perplex Fenwick are related, and philosophers declining thoroughly to probe these marvels, they have been abandoned for the most part to persons who know little or nothing of philosophy or metaphysics, and remain insoluble."[40] Through *Story* Bulwer sought to encourage philosophers to inquire into these marvels as Bacon, Newton, and Davy would have done. "There must be," he told Forster, "a natural cause for them—if they are not purely imposture."[41] He ended his letter affirming his belief in the substance of what used to be called magic, arguing his familiar notion about magical powers residing in persons of peculiar temperaments—the thesis he advanced in "The Haunted and the Haunters."

For all the magic in *A Strange Story*—an elixir of life and immortality; mind control achieved with conjuring wands, mesmerism and clairvoyance, and witchcraft and alchemy in the closing cauldron scene—Bulwer's book is not a romantic novel like *Zanoni* because it contains no arguments supporting the ideal in art. And unlike *Zanoni*, *Story* advances no political message. Instead, it espouses a religious thesis that combats materialism and Darwinism by illustrating through the spiritual reeducation of the story's hero (Dr. Allen Fenwick) the existence and immortality of the human soul.

A doctrinaire philosophical materialist, Fenwick repudiates those who accept with credulity what they cannot explain by reason, including a belief in God and the existence of a human soul. Whatever knowledge we possess, Fenwick claims, we owe solely to nature. But to Bulwer such philosophies, in rejecting healthful creeds and in undermining religious faith, only invent systems more complex than the mysteries of theology. These philosophers, Bulwer argues, would leave nothing in the universe but their own vain delusions. They are guilty of impiety and intellectual presumption. The power of the novel's controlling bildungsroman plot—one in which science comes to the support of orthodox Christian beliefs—rests on Fenwick's hard-won discovery that man has a soul and that some things cannot be explained by reason alone. At the novel's close Fenwick freely acknowledges Christianity as the only true faith and the Bible and prayer as the only way to find salvation. In Fenwick's conversion Bulwer provides evidence for the soul's existence, arguing that among animals only man possesses the capacity to conceive of God. To Bulwer this special attribute furnishes a vigorous repudiation of the Darwinian view of evolution.

As Bulwer feared, the reviews of *A Strange Story* proved generally hostile. The *Eclectic Review*, a nonconformist periodical, applauded the novel as a reaffirmation of Christianity. The reviewer saw the book as "a protest against the intrusion of man into hidden mysteries" and approved of Bulwer's use of the supernatural "as indispensable to . . . romantic narratives."[42] *A Strange Story*, he continued, illustrated a "healthy change" in moral tone from Bulwer's earlier novels, which exerted "a pernicious influence" on the reader.[43]

In contrast, the *Athenaeum* reviewer felt that the book's "magic and science, poetry and prose, meet . . . in a sort of witch-dance."[44] Bulwer's novel, he thought, would only torment the reader who had not "eaten of the insane root" of the author's wayward imagination.[45] He found the dialogue unconvincing and strongly objected to the didactic passages that interfered with the story. In sum, the novel was "too stagey, and too contrived."[46] The *Saturday Review* wondered why Bulwer returned to the supernatural mode so many years after *Zanoni,* having succeeded so well with his domestic novels in the Caxton series. The preface, the reviewer complained, "obtrudes itself clamorously upon the reader's notice" and was hard work for the average reader.[47] He believed the story "extremely ugly," liking nothing in the book but the character of Mrs. Poyntz.[48] Even the usually complimentary *Examiner* seemed more dutiful in its review than enthusiastic. The critic accepted the validity of Bulwer's use of the occult, saw Margrave's character as original, praised the cauldron scene, approved of the Faber-Fenwick conversations, and liked Mrs. Poyntz, but did not laud the book as a great work of fiction.[49]

Bulwer was greatly disappointed by the reviews. He wrote his son complaining that the public disliked mysticism and allegory. He believed *Story* his "highest, though not [his] broadest work, of prose fiction," but he felt the novel "hurt" his reputation because of the "impertinent" reviews it received.[50]

The Coming Race as a Condemnation of Advanced Ideas

The Coming Race—Bulwer's cautionary romance about an advanced society in the earth's interior—should be grouped with *The Parisians* (1873) and *Kenelm Chillingly* (1873), as all three share a similar theme and moral purpose. In each Bulwer expostulates against the popularity of social and political theories that he thought undermined individual character and national life. He completed *The Coming Race* in March 1870 and sent it to John Forster for his opinion. Forster liked it, returning the manuscript with only a few suggestions pencilled in the margins. Appearing anonymously, *The Coming Race* was published in one volume by Blackwood in early spring 1871 and dedicated to Professor Max Müller as a token of Bulwer's respect and admiration. *Race* proved popular with both the public and critics, running to five editions the first year alone. Such popularity surprised Bulwer, who earlier predicted to his friend Lady Sherborne that the novel would have only a limited appeal.[51] To his son Bulwer wrote on 30 January 1872 that *Race* owed its success to "the praise of the reviewers . . . who would have been most uncivil to the author . . . had they guessed [his identity]."[52] The idea for *Race* first appeared some thirty-five years earlier in "Asmodeus at Large," a satiric piece published in his miscellany, *The Student* (1835).

In *Race* Bulwer sought to describe a society in which most of the utopian philosophies of his day were fully realized. Peace, prosperity, personal liberty, full social equality of sex and class, scientific mastery over nature, great technological innovation, perfect physical well-being, and complete communal harmony produced a race of people mild yet terrible, bright but remarkably dull. Bulwer intended his scientific romance to go beyond mere fantasy and adventure. He wrote his son in June 1871 outlining the book's two artistic aims. If all the utopian dreams for human society could be achieved, he speculated, the result would be "firstly, a race . . . fatal to ourselves; our society could not amalgamate with it; it would be deadly to us, not from its vices but its virtue. Secondly, the realisation of these ideas would produce a society which we should find extremely dull, and in which the current equality would prohibit all greatness."[53] Writing against the background of civil turmoil in France (the Commune), Bulwer wanted to show the dangers of social leveling and utopian attempts to remold human nature.

By classification *The Coming Race* is an anti-utopian novel, an adventure story, a tale of wonderful discovery, a conservative sociopolitical satire, and a cautionary apologue reminding us of the inherent limits of the human species. The novel's broad satire pillories democracy as the rule of the most ignorant, attacks socialism as universal "strife-rot," associates women's equality with blatant moral looseness, and burlesques Darwinism as a debate on whether man or ape is the final product of evolution. But these formulas give place to the novel's shaping thesis that should we ever fulfill all our dreams of perfectibility and achieve an earthly paradise based on a better, higher, and calmer sphere of being, our very nature—thriving on competition, ambition, self-interest, lust for power, and desire for personal distinction—would prevent us from enjoying such a beatified community. In short order, Bulwer claims, we would either die of boredom or undermine the good of the community by our destructive urges. A perfectly ordered civilization annuls the motives of individuals long conditioned by contest and struggle, militating against any form of human greatness. Without this impetus to high aspiration, society would produce no great soldiers and statesmen, no great orators and thinkers, and no great works of art. As a consequence, Bulwer urges us to remain content with our present condition and not strive for what we are unfit by nature to achieve, sustain, or enjoy.

As an apologue, *The Coming Race* features little development of character because the book stresses ideas rather than people. Of the half dozen named characters in the novel—Zee, Tae, Aph-Lin, Bra, Lo, and Tish—only the American narrator (Tish) has any importance as a character. He both describes and reacts to the wonders he sees like a nineteenth-century Gulliver, awed by Vril-ya society but compelled by racial pride to portray his own world as favorably as possible. In doing so, he serves as the butt of Bulwer's satire against American thought and behavior. Tish dramatizes what Bulwer believes to be the inconsistency in the American national character— a fondness for social rank and a penchant for democratic leveling.

In his occult fiction Bulwer achieved genuine distinction not only as a pioneer in the genre, but also as one of its most brilliant practitioners. *Zanoni* was his masterpiece, closely followed in artistic merit by *A Strange Story*. The two novels are a vade mecum of the occult and esoteric traditions. But magic and mysticism served as the means to greater ends, providing Bulwer with an ideal vehicle to attack materialism, Marxism, and Darwinism. By employing occult themes Bulwer sought not to titillate the public's interest in the sensational, but rather to find a useful form in which to discuss advanced ideas of the age. "The Haunted and the Haunters" was one of the best short occult stories written in the Victorian period, remaining as fresh and thrilling today as when it was first conceived. In *The Coming Race* Bulwer created a dystopia that in its vision and imagination surpassed the work of many of the scientific romancers of the 1890s, including Fred White, Grant Allen, and George Griffith. During the 1890s, when occult fiction flowered in England, writers as different in approach as Frances E. Trollope, Florence Marryat, and Sir Henry Rider Haggard were able to build upon the foundations Bulwer laid in the genre some forty years earlier.

Chapter Eight
The Question of Bulwer's Achievement

Distinguished as a novelist, dramatist, poet, scholar, editor, member of Parliament, and cabinet minister, Bulwer possessed a universality of talents and interests that is underscored by the number and quality of his published works. His canon of writings is impressive, especially as he wrote in a literary age noted for its energy and high productivity. He published fifty-nine major works during the seventy years of his life—thirty novels, some three dozen stories, fourteen plays, nine volumes of poetry, and more than a dozen volumes of miscellaneous prose (magazine articles, translations, and historical studies).

Bulwer was one of the few Victorian novelists to write for the theater successfully. Of his fourteen carefully designed plays, nine were staged and printed, and two, *The Lady of Lyons* (1838) and *Money* (1840), were enormously popular and frequently revived. In fact, *Money* was selected for a gala performance at Drury Lane on 17 May 1911 in honor of the German emperor's visit for the coronation of King George V.[1] Equally distinguished is Bulwer's *England and the English* (1833), his brilliant social history of nineteenth-century England in transition, which, in its scope and analysis, is the equal of R. H. Horne's *New Spirit of the Age* (1844) and Alexis de Tocqueville's *Democracy in America* (1835–40). But it was chiefly as a novelist that Bulwer achieved his fame, and any final assessment of his standing must focus primarily on this branch of literature. As Bulwer so often claimed, he wrote less for his own age than for the coming one. By his own admission, he believed that future readers would rightly judge his books, recognize his merits, and vindicate his literary reputation. How has he fared with readers in an age far removed from the Victorian era?

Among his thirty novels, Bulwer produced a dozen that recent critics agree are works of genuine literary distinction: *Pelham* (1828), *Paul Clifford* (1830), *Zanoni* (1842), *The Last of the Barons* (1843),

Harold (1848), *The Caxtons* (1849), *My Novel* (1853), *A Strange Story* (1862), *The Coming Race* (1871), *The Parisians* (1873), *Kenelm Chillingly* (1873), and the tale "The Haunted and the Haunters" (1859). Four of these works—*Pelham, Zanoni, My Novel,* and "Haunted"— are his masterpieces because of their powerful ideas, their vast learning, and their compositional brilliance.

Bulwer's chief merit as a novelist rests on the power of his intellect and on the fertility of his imagination. His best novels contain a rich store of information; their recurring subject is the study of characters who represent different intellectual positions. The novels establish Bulwer as an essentially intellectual writer and not a mere storyteller and weaver of plots. Each novel seeks to engage the reader's mind and to air important issues, ranging from Benthamism and political reform to ideas in history, the sciences, and the arts. As their dates of publication affirm, Bulwer's books show no decline in his artistic or intellectual powers at the end of his career. On the contrary, nearly half of his best novels were written in the latter part of his career—three in the last four years of his life.

If his chief assets were his intellect and imagination, Bulwer's most reconizable fault lay in his writing style. This defect is manifested in his occasional tendency to use elaborate phrases and constructions, to employ grandiloquent and antique modes of expression, and to prefer noble-sounding names and titles. These mannerisms led Bulwer into that "premeditated fine writing" that so infuriated Thackeray.[2] But Bulwer's "fine writing," like that of his contemporaries, was mainly a response to reader expectations in an age demanding refined genteelisms in fiction.

Another of Bulwer's failings was his inability to draw women effectively in his novels. Many of his female characters are merely stage heroines rather than critical studies of human nature.[3] This stemmed in part from the ideal conception of womanhood he fashioned out of his boyhood romances. Nearly all his heroines have the same idealized attributes; they are fairy-like innocents untouched by either conventional education or morality. Such idealizations helped to earn Bulwer his reputation as a racy, dangerous writer, as some of his fictional heroines led morally suspect lives. Generally, they were modeled on Lucy D——, his first romantic love, or on Lady Caroline Lamb. Only in his portraits of Lizzie Morley *(The Parisians)* and Mrs. Colonel Poyntz *(A Strange Story)* did he fully succeed in creating convincing female characters.

Despite these shortcomings, Bulwer's fiction exerted a powerful influence on his contemporaries and successors alike. *Pelham,* his first spectacular success, created a myth of fashionable life that provided the formal design for many silver-fork novels written after 1828. As Allan Christensen noted, Bulwer made "the fashionable world possible for art" by placing Almacks at the center of a futile society around which "Certain stereotypes of social climbers, dandies, and bored women" revolved.[4] His portrait of Henry Pelham as "an outrageously flippant and cynical dandy aristocrat, who nevertheless had a hidden social conscience and who was utterly dedicated to noble political and aesthetic ideals," provided the silver-fork novel with its most enduring image of the fashionable hero.[5] After *Pelham*'s publication, many silver-fork novelists—namely, T. H. Lister, Robert Plumer Ward, Theodore Hook, Mrs. Catherine Gore, Lady Charlotte Bury, the Countess of Blessington, and Benjamin Disraeli—incorporated Bulwer's design and his dandified hero into their novels.

Bulwer's influence on Disraeli's silver-fork novels was a direct one. He read and criticized Disraeli's *The Young Duke* (1831) in manuscript, giving him useful literary advice. The tighter design and greater coherence in Disraeli's *Contarini Fleming* (1832) and *Henrietta Temple* (1837) stem directly from Bulwer's surer sense of compositional art. Sarah Bradford claims that the young Disraeli modeled his public conduct upon the eccentricities of Henry Pelham. His later social successes he attributed, in Christensen's phrase, to having "pelhamized" people.[6] *Pelham* is the best of some three dozen or so silver-fork novels published between 1820 and 1847. Ernest A. Baker thought it a better book than Dirsaeli's equally influential *Vivian Grey* (1826–27).[7]

Bulwer's first Newgate novel, *Paul Clifford* (1830), proved equally influential to the development of Victorian crime fiction. In it he attacked the penal laws and argued that crime arose as often from environment (poverty and lack of education) as from moral flaws in character. Allan Christensen claims that Bulwer's commitment in *Paul Clifford* to "noble political and social causes" opened "a new field for the contemporary novel."[8] Other early Victorian novelists rushed to imitate Bulwer's crime thrillers, but they usually copied his sensationalism rather than his social criticism or metaphysical approach. One of these imitators was William Harrison Ainsworth, who in *Rookwood* (1834) and in *Jack Sheppard* (1839) employed most of the components in Bulwer's Newgate formula: the highwayman as a romantic antihero, criminal slang, "flash" songs, safehouses, and cave hideouts.

Far more influential than *Paul Clifford* was Bulwer's second Newgate thriller, *Eugene Aram* (1832), which was a psychological case study of the criminal mind. Its direct influence can be traced in Wilkie Collins's portrait of his master criminal, Count Fosco, in the enormously popular *The Woman in White* (1859–60). In *Night and Morning* (1841)—Bulwer's indictment of the distinctions society makes between working-class crime and well-heeled vice—he influenced the mid-Victorian novel of social protest. Such an influence can be found in Charles Reade's two tendenzromane, *It Is Never Too Late to Mend* (1856) and *Hard Cash* (1863), whose prison scenes and reform programs echo Bulwer's thesis in *Night and Morning*.

In Bulwer's bildungsromane, or novels of initiation and self-education, he built on and expanded Goethe's bildung pattern in *Wilhelm Meister* (1796). While Thomas Carlyle published a translation of Goethe's novel in 1824, Bulwer was the first to employ this pattern in a work of English fiction. He expanded the three-part bildungsroman plot (the hero's rebellion, quest, and attainment of self-knowledge), and gave the formula many of its modern-day variations. Through *Ernest Maltravers* (1837) and *Alice* (1838), he managed to influence Dickens, who used the pattern in *David Copperfield* (1849–50) and *Great Expectations* (1860–61). Such a link is clearly established by Dickens and Bulwer's frequent exchange of ideas about their fiction in progress. The second ending that Dickens wrote for *Great Expectations* came directly from Bulwer's suggestions for an alternative ending to Pip's story of initiation. Thackeray also built upon Bulwer's bildungsroman formula in *Pendennis* (1848–50) and *The Newcomes* (1853–55). In 1848 he told Lady Blessington that in Bulwer's novels "there are big words which make me furious, and a pretentious fine writing against which I can't help rebelling."[9] Yet as Ellen Moers notes, "Thackeray's early diary testifies to the closeness with which he followed Bulwer's exclusive rise to fame, and the care with which he read *Falkland, The Disowned, Pelham, Devereux,* and so on."[10] In the hero of *Pendennis,* Allan Christensen recognized "an upsidedown Pelham" as well as Thackeray's first attempt to use Bulwer's novel-of-initiation formula.[11]

Despite being Sir Walter Scott's most talented successor in historical fiction, Bulwer exerted little influence upon his immediate contemporaries working in the genre. Costume romancers like William Harrison Ainsworth, G. P. R. James, and Horace Smith copied Scott's least successful Waverley novels, emphasizing, as Scott had done in his potboilers, romance and picturesque effects rather than concentrated historical analysis. To some extent, Ainsworth's painstaking documentation reflects Bulwer's call for greater historical accuracy, but Ainsworth seldom went beyond accurate descriptions of period architecture and furniture. Bulwer's more scholarly approach did, however, strongly influence a later generation of Victorian writers. His demand for more rigorous historical interpretation is seen in Charles Kingsley's *Westward Ho* (1855) and in Charles Reade's *The Cloister and the Hearth* (1861). In these two novels picturesque effects give place to sustained analysis of the forces shaping Elizabethan England and pre-Reformation Holland. Kingsley's *Hypatia* (1853) and *Hereward the Wake* (1865) show the thematic and methodological influence of Bulwer's *The Last Days of Pompeii* (1834) and *Harold* (1848), respectively. George Eliot's *Romola* (1862–63), Joseph Henry Shorthouse's *John Inglesant* (1880), and William Morris's *The Dream of John Ball* (1888) continued Bulwer's historical approach, establishing him as an important link between Scott and later Victorian historical novelists.

Aside from his silver-fork novels of the 1820s, Bulwer did not write any domestic fiction until 1849. It may be argued that *The Caxtons* (1849) and *My Novel* (1853), with their rural settings and their focus on country squires and parsons, influenced Anthony Trollope at the beginning of his career. Told by a publisher that historical novels were out of fashion, Trollope abandoned historical fiction and turned to domestic realism. In his Barsetshire novels he used the same settings and character types that Bulwer had already portrayed so successfully in his popular Caxton series. The Australian scenes at the close of *The Caxtons* created a new fictional genre, the colonial novel. Coral Lansbury believes that the colonial propaganda written by Samuel Sidney was the source of Bulwer's myth of Australia as a "blessed land in which experience chastened and redeemed" the prodigal who returned "to England and to harmony with himself."[12]

Bulwer's use of this myth directly influenced Dickens, who sent the irrepressible Wilkins Micawber to Australia at the close of *David Copperfield* (1849–50) to retrieve his fortunes and mend his ways. In its design and theme, Henry Kingsley's *Geoffry Hamlyn* (1859) also owes much to the Australian myth in *The Caxtons*. In addition, Bulwer's *A Strange Story* (1862), which featured thrilling scenes in the Australian bush, influenced modern Australian fiction. Echoes of *The Caxtons* and *A Strange Story* are found in the "bush ranger" novels of Fergus Hume, Rolf Boldrewood, and Marcus Clarke. The Bulwerian myth of Australia as the land of personal salvation may be seen in Henry Handel Richardson's *The Fortunes of Richard Mahony* trilogy (1917–29).

Bulwer's occult and scientific romances had both a short- and a long-term influence on the supernatural and occult novel genres. The revival of supernatural fiction during the late 1840s—represented by the publication of Ainsworth's *The Lancashire Witches* (1848–49), Prest-Rymer's *Varney the Vampyre* (1847), and G. W. M. Reynolds's *Faust* (1845–46), *Wagner the Wehr-Wolf* (1846–47), and *The Necromancer* (1851–52)—must be attributed to the great popularity of Bulwer's *Zanoni* (1842). During the 1890s, Bulwer's occult novels helped to lay the foundations for the revival of the occult novel in England. His influence is especially noted in the occult fiction of Florence Marryat, Vernon Lee, Amelia Edwards, Frances E. Trollope, and Benjamin Leopold Farjeon. Equally significant is Bulwer's influence on Sir Henry Rider Haggard's *King Solomon's Mines* (1885) and its sequel, *She* (1886–87), in which Haggard updated Bulwer's use of the immortalist theme and the Ayesha myth. In *The Coming Race* (1871), Bulwer produced an important conservative dystopia and one of the best scientific romances before the florescence of science fiction during the 1890s. Its dramatization of the horrors of a perfect society generated a reply in Samuel Butler's *Erewhon* (1872) and its sequel, *Erewhon Revisited* (1901). In his scientific romance *Looking Backward* (1888), Edward Bellamy argued a radical thesis in response to Bulwer's conservative utopian satire. He portrayed a future world in which universal peace and prosperity are achieved through worldwide socialist cooperation, a view Bulwer would have strongly rejected.

Despite his widespread influence on others, Bulwer failed to attain the first rank as a novelist. In 1830, before Dickens and Thackeray began to write, he was the most original and important novelist in England. Today, he is assessed by historians of the novel as the best of the younger generation of novelists who commenced their writing careers in the 1820s—novelists like Frederick Marryat, G. P. R. James, William Harrison Ainsworth, Charles Lever, Theodore Hook,

George Robert Gleig, Horace Smith, and R. S. Surtees. While Bulwer's novels fall short of those written by the major nineteenth-century writers (Austen, Scott, Dickens, Thackeray, Charlotte Brontë, Eliot, Meredith, and Hardy), Bulwer easily belongs to the next level of novelists. Based on the consummate artistry and intellectual power in his best novels, he can be ranked with writers like Benjamin Disraeli, Anthony Trollope, Elizabeth Gaskell, George Gissing, George Moore, and Mrs. Humphry Ward. Like them, Bulwer wrote a number of good novels but failed to produce books of the consistently high artistic level necessary to be rated a major novelist. Still victim of a bad press,[13] his writings warrant serious study, and if they are closely read, they will repay modern readers by their impressive erudition and their remarkable compositional skill. Bulwer believed that "to have served his own generation in a higher or lower sphere is a glorious description of any man's life."[14] The judgment of recent Bulwer scholarship suggests that he attained the higher rather than the lower sphere in his art.

Notes and References

Chapter One

    1. Wilkie Collins, *Basil*, vol. 10 of *The Works of Wilkie Collins* (New York: P. F. Collier, n.d.), 5.

    2. Victor Alexander Lytton, second earl of Lytton, *The Life of Edward Bulwer, First Lord Lytton*, by His Grandson, 2 vols., (London, 1913), 1:102–03.

    3. Ibid., 1:36.

    4. Ibid.

    5. Ibid., 1:45.

    6. Ibid., 1:56.

    7. Ibid., 1:83 ff.

    8. Ibid., 1:61.

    9. Ibid., 1:83.

    10. Ibid., 1:122.

    11. Ibid.

    12. Ibid., 1:134.

    13. Ibid., 1:157.

    14. Victor Lytton, *Life*, 1:184 ff.

    15. Ibid., 1:207.

    16. Ibid., 1:219.

    17. Ibid., 1:248.

    18. Victor Lytton, *Bulwer-Lytton*, 34.

    19. Victor Lytton, *Life*, 1:249.

    20. Victor Lytton, *Bulwer-Lytton*, 34.

    21. Ibid., 34–35.

    22. Ibid., 35.

    23. Ibid.

    24. Ibid., 36.

    25. Ibid., 36–37.

    26. Ibid., 53–58.

    27. Ibid., 62.

    28. Ibid.

    29. Ibid., 63.

    30. Ibid.

    31. Ibid.

    32. Ibid., 63–64.

    33. Ibid., 64.

    34. Victor Lytton, *Life*, 2:280–96.

35. Ibid., 2:270.
36. Ibid., 2:279.
37. Ibid., 2:309.
38. Ibid., 2:355.
39. Ibid., 2:487.
40. Victor Lytton, *Bulwer-Lytton*, 107.

Chapter Two

1. Robert Lytton, first earl of Lytton, *The Life, Letters, and Literary Remains of Edward Bulwer, Lord Lytton, by His Son*, 2 vols. (New York: Harper and Brothers, 1884), 1:386–87.

2. To Rosina Doyle Wheeler, 1826, in Victor Lytton, *Life*, 1:185.

3. Victor Lytton, *Life*, 1:186.

4. Ibid., 1:187.

5. Michael Sadleir, *Bulwer: A Panorama: Edward and Rosina, 1803–1836* (Boston, 1931), 170.

6. *Falkland*, 1st novel library ed. with introduction by Park Honan (London: Cassell, 1967), 27. Subsequent references cited in the text.

7. Robert Lytton, *Life, Letters, and Literary Remains*, 1:491.

8. Sadleir, *Bulwer*, 173.

9. To Mrs. Edward Bulwer, 2 February 1828, in Louisa Devey, *The Letters of the Late Edward Bulwer, Lord Lytton, to His Wife* (New York, 1889; rpt., New York: AMS, 1976), 329–30.

10. Robert Lytton, *Life, Letters, and Literary Remains*, 1:486n.

11. Ibid., 1:488.

12. Jerome Hamilton Buckley, *Season of Youth: The Bildungsroman from Dickens to Golding* (Cambridge, 1974), 17–18.

13. *Pelham*, Illustrated Library Edition (Boston and New York: Colonial Press Co., n.d.), 4. Subsequent references cited in the text.

14. Robert Lytton, *Life, Letters, and Literary Remains*, 1:504.

15. Sadleir, *Bulwer*, 191.

16. Robert Lytton, *Life, Letters, and Literary Remains*, 1:506.

17. Ibid.

18. Ibid.

19. Ibid.

20. Ibid., 1:506–7.

21. *The Disowned*, Illustrated Library Edition (Boston and New York: Colonial Press Co., n.d.), 459.

22. Sadleir, *Bulwer*, 191.

23. The manuscript of *Greville* is printed in Robert Lytton, *Life, Letters, and Literary Remains*, 1:621–64.

24. Ibid., 1:657.

25. *Devereux,* Illustrated Library Edition (Boston and New York: Colonial Press Co., n.d.), vi. Subsequent references cited in the text.

26. Sadleir, *Bulwer,* 202.

Chapter Three

1. Victor Lytton, *Bulwer-Lytton,* 43.

2. Sadleir, *Bulwer,* 208n.

3. Ibid., 207.

4. Keith Hollingsworth, *The Newgate Novel, 1830–1847: Bulwer, Ainsworth, Dickens, and Thackeray* (Detroit, 1963), 14.

5. Besides Bulwer's four Newgate romances, other popular novels in the Newgate tradition were: Charles Dickens's *Oliver Twist* (1838) and *Barnaby Rudge* (1841), William Harrison Ainsworth's *Rookwood* (1834) and *Jack Sheppard* (1839), Mrs. Frances Sheridan's *Carwell* (1830), Theodore Hook's *Maxwell* (1830), Horace Smith's *Gale Middleton* (1833), Charles Whitehead's *Jack Ketch* (1833), William Mudford's *Stephen Dugard* (1841), Catherine Crowe's *Susan Hopley* (1841), and William Makepeace Thackeray's anti-Newgate novel *Catherine* (1839–40).

6. Hollingsworth, *Newgate Novel,* 14–15.

7. Ibid., pp. 71–72.

8. *Paul Clifford,* Illustrated Library Edition (Boston and New York: Colonial Press Co., n.d.), 78–79. Subsequent references cited in the text.

9. Sadleir, *Bulwer,* 207.

10. Hollingsworth, *Newgate Novel,* 74.

11. Ibid., 78–82.

12. Ibid., 80.

13. Victor Lytton, *Bulwer-Lytton,* 46.

14. Hollingsworth, *Newgate Novel,* 81.

15. Ibid.

16. Ibid., 82.

17. Victor Lytton, *Life,* 1:364.

18. Thomas Hay Sweet Escott, *Edward Bulwer, First Baron Lytton of Knebworth: A Social, Personal, and Political Monograph* (London, 1910), 176–77.

19. Ibid., 125.

20. Victor Lytton, *Life,* 1:387–88.

21. *Eugene Aram,* Illustrated Library Edition (Boston and New York: Colonial Press Co., n.d.), 1831 Preface, xiii. Subsequent references cited in the text.

22. Hollingsworth, *Newgate Novel,* 91.

23. Ibid., 93.

24. Ibid.

25. Ibid.

26. Ibid., 96.

27. Victor Lytton, *Life,* 1:389.

28. *Night and Morning,* Illustrated Library Edition (Boston and New York: Colonial Press Co., n.d.), x. Subsequent references cited in the text.

29. Hollingsworth, *Newgate Novel,* 174.

30. Ibid.

31. Ibid.

32. Ibid., 171.

33. Victor Lytton, *Bulwer-Lytton,* 88.

34. *Lucretia; or, The Children of Night,* Illustrated Library Edition (Boston and New York: Colonial Press, Co., n.d.), v. Subsequent references cited in the text.

35. Victor Lytton, *Life,* 1:86n.

36. Hollingsworth, *Newgate Novel,* 191.

37. Ibid., 193.

38. Ibid., 194.

39. Ibid., 196.

40. Ibid., 196–97.

41. Ibid., 200.

42. Ibid., 192.

Chapter Four

1. Victor Lytton, *Life,* 1:363–64.

2. Edwin M. Eigner, *The Metaphysical Novel in England and America: Dickens, Bulwer, Hawthorne, Melville* (Berkeley, 1978), 58.

3. Ibid.

4. Ibid., 2.

5. Ibid., 3.

6. Ibid.

7. Ibid., 4.

8. Ibid.

9. Ibid., 5.

10. Ibid.

11. Ibid., 7.

12. Ibid.

13. Preface to 1840 edition, *Godolphin,* Illustrated Library Edition (Boston and New York: Colonial Press Co., n.d.), viii. Subsequent references cited in the text.

14. Sadleir, *Bulwer,* 283–84.

15. Victor Lytton, *Bulwer-Lytton,* 48.

16. Allan Conrad Christensen, *Edward Bulwer-Lytton: The Fiction of New Regions* (Athens, Ga., 1976), 78–79.

17. Ibid.

18. *The Pilgrims of the Rhine,* Illustrated Library Edition (Boston and New York: Colonial Press, Co., n.d.), vii. Hereafter cited as *Pilgrims.* Subsequent references cited in the text.

19. Sadleir, *Bulwer,* 279.

20. *Ernest Maltravers,* Illustrated Library Edition (Boston and New York: Colonial Press, n.d.) "Preface 1837 edition," ix. Hereafter cited as *Maltravers.* Subsequent references cited in the text.

21. *Alice; or, The Mysteries,* Illustrated Library Edition (Boston and New York: Colonial Press, n.d.), XI.VIII.445. Subsequent references cited in the text.

22. Prefatory note, *The Parisians* (London, Glasgow, and Manchester: George Routledge and Sons, 1891), vi. Subsequent references cited in the text.

23. Victor Lytton, *Bulwer-Lytton,* 101.

24. Prefatory Note to *The Parisians,* v.

25. To Mrs. Conway Halliday, 9 September 1872, in Victor Lytton, *Life,* 2:481.

26. Victor Lytton, *Bulwer-Lytton,* 100.

Chapter Five

1. *Blackwood's Edinburgh Magazine* 58 (September 1845):341.

2. *Westminster Review* 45 (1846):35.

3. Andrew Sanders, *The Victorian Historical Novel, 1840–1880* (London and Basingstoke, 1978), 11.

4. *Monthly Chronicle* 1 (1838):138–39.

5. Ibid., 42–43.

6. Ibid., 43.

7. Ibid., 44.

8. Sadleir, *Bulwer,* 332.

9. James C. Simmons, "Bulwer and Vesuvius: The Topicality of *The Last Days of Pompeii,*" *Nineteenth-Century Fiction* 24 (June 1969): 103–5.

10. Curtis Dahl, "Edward Bulwer-Lytton," in *Victorian Fiction: A Second Guide to Research,* ed. George H. Ford, (New York, 1978), 33.

11. Preface to the 1834 edition, *The Last Days of Pompeii* (London, Glasgow, and Manchester: George Routledge and Sons, 1891), ii. Hereafter cited as *Pompeii.* Subsequent references cited in the text.

12. Bulwer's concern about sectarianism and the evangelical movement is reflected by other novelists of the period. Andrew Picken's *The Sectarian; or, The Church and the Meeting House* (1829) and James Hogg's *Memoirs and Confessions of a Justified Sinner* (1824) treat similar themes.

13. Sadleir, *Bulwer,* 334.

14. Victor Lytton, *Life,* 1:444.

15. Ibid., 1:444–45.

16. Ibid., 1:446–47.

17. Preface to 1835 edition, *Rienzi; or, The Last of the Roman Tribunes* (London, Glasgow, and Manchester: George Routledge and Sons, 1891), vii. Subsequent references cited in the text.

18. Robert Lytton, *Life, Letters, and Literary Remains,* 1:441.

19. Sadleir, *Bulwer,* 336.

20. Ibid.

21. *Leila; or, The Siege of Granada* (Boston and New York: Colonial Press, Co., n.d.), i. Subsequent references cited in the text.

22. *Calderon the Courtier: A Tale* (Boston and New York: Colonial Press Co., n.d.), 5:318–19. Subsequent references cited in the text.

23. Preface to 1843 edition, *The Last of the Barons* (London, Glasgow, and Manchester: George Routledge and Sons, 1891), xxii. Subsequent references cited in the text.

24. Dedicatory epistle to 1848 edition, *Harold, the Last of the Saxon Kings* (London, Glasgow, and Manchester: George Routledge and Sons, 1891), v. Subsequent references cited in the text.

25. "On the Spirit in Which New Theories Should Be Received," in *Caxtoniana: A Series of Essays on Life, Literature, and Manners* (New York: Harper and Brothers, 1864), 138.

26. Sanders, *Victorian Historical Novel,* 65.

27. Ibid.

28. Ibid.

29. Ibid.

30. Ibid.

31. Ibid.

32. Ibid., 57.

33. Dedication to 1876 edition, *Pausanias the Spartan: An Unfinished Historical Romance* (Boston and New York: Colonial Press Co., n.d.), 182. Subsequent references cited in the text.

34. Lionel Stevenson, *The English Novel: A Panorama* (Boston: 1960), 255.

Chapter Six

1. Victor Lytton, *Life,* 2:104.

2. Christensen, *Edward Bulwer-Lytton,* 137.

3. Ibid.

4. Ibid., 139.

5. Victor Lytton, *Life,* 2:398.

6. Ibid., 2:399.

7. Ibid.

8. *Caxtoniana,* 197.

Notes and References

141

9. Ibid.

10. Victor Lytton, *Life,* 2:127.

11. Ibid.

12. Ibid., 2:161.

13. Christensen, *Edward Bulwer-Lytton,* 138.

14. Victor Lytton, *Life,* 2:119.

15. Ibid., 2:129.

16. Ibid., 105. "Maga" was the nickname given to *Blackwood's Magazine.*

17. Ibid., 2:106.

18. Preface (1853) to *Lucretia,* v.

19. Ibid.

20. Ibid.

21. Preface, *The Caxtons: A Family Picture* (Boston and New York: Colonial Press Co., n.d.), v. Subsequent references cited in the text.

22. Escott, *Edward Bulwer,* 273–76.

23. Walter E. Houghton, ed., *The Wellesley Index to Victorian Periodicals, 1824–1900* (Toronto and London, 1966), 1:8–9.

24. Escott, *Edward Bulwer,* 298.

25. *My Novel by Pisistratus Caxton; or, Varieties in English Life* (Boston: Colonial Press Co., n.d.), i. Subsequent references cited in the text.

26. Ernest A. Baker, *The History of the English Novel: The Age of Dickens and Thackeray* (London, 1936), 7:197–98.

27. Ibid., 7:198.

28. Ibid.

29. See Barry Qualls's *The Secular Pilgrims of Victorian Fiction: The Novel as Book of Life* (Cambridge, 1982), 15–16, for an account of Bulwer's part in creating a secular myth of human spiritual progress in Victorian fiction.

30. "On Certain Principles of Art in Works of Imagination," in *Caxtoniana,* 319.

31. Robert Louis Stevenson, "A Gossip on Romance," in *Collected Works* (New York: Davos Press, 1906), 6:120.

32. Victor Lytton, *Life,* 2:250.

33. Ibid., 2:251.

34. Escott, *Edward Bulwer,* 4.

35. *What Will He Do with It?* (Boston and New York: Colonial Press Co., n.d.), 3:3.156. Subsequent references cited in the text.

36. Baker, *History,* 7:200.

37. Victor Lytton, *Bulwer-Lytton,* 93.

38. Ibid.

Chapter Seven

    1. Victor Lytton, *Life,* 2:41.

    2. Ibid.

    3. Ibid., 2:40.

    4. Ibid., 2:41.

    5. Ibid.

    6. Ibid., 2:40.

    7. Ibid.

    8. Robert Lee Wolff, *Strange Stories and Other Explorations in Victorian Fiction* (Boston, 1971), 158.

    9. Ibid., 154.

    10. Victor Lytton, *Life,* 2:32.

    11. *Zanoni* (Boston and New York: Colonial Press Co., n.d.), 1. Subsequent references cited in the text.

    12. Victor Lytton, *Life,* 2:34–35.

    13. Wolff, *Strange Stories,* 217.

    14. Ibid., 161.

    15. Ibid., 224–25.

    16. Victor Lytton, *Life,* 2:51.

    17. Wolff, *Strange Stories,* 202.

    18. Ibid.

    19. Ibid., 203.

    20. Ibid., 204.

    21. Ibid., 205.

    22. Ibid.

    23. Ibid.

    24. Ibid.

    25. Ibid., 206.

    26. Ibid., 207.

    27. Ibid., 205.

    28. Christensen, *Edward Bulwer-Lytton,* 234.

    29. Escott, *Edward Bulwer,* 301.

    30. Mme. Dunglas Home, *The Gift of D. D. Home* (London: Kegan Paul, Trench, Trubner, 1890), 35–36.

    31. "The Haunted and the Haunters," in *The Caxtons* (Boston and New York: Colonial Press Co., n.d.), 311. Subsequent references cited in the text.

    32. Victor Lytton, *Life,* 2:340–41.

    33. Ibid., 2:343–44.

    34. Ibid., 2:344–45.

    35. *A Strange Story* (Boston and New York: Colonial Press, Co., n.d.), Preface, vi. Subsequent references cited in the text.

    36. Victor Lytton, *Life,* 2:346.

37. Ibid.
38. Ibid.
39. Ibid.
40. Ibid., 2:47.
41. Ibid.
42. Wolff, *Strange Stories*, 301.
43. Ibid., 303.
44. Ibid., 303.
45. Ibid.
46. Ibid.
47. Ibid., 303–4.
48. Ibid., 304.
49. Ibid.
50. Ibid., 306.
51. Victor Lytton, *Life*, 2:468.
52. Ibid., 2:469.
53. Ibid., 2:468.

Chapter Eight

1. Victor Lytton, *Bulwer-Lytton*, 73.
2. Victor Lytton, *Life*, 2:494.
3. Ibid., 2:498.
4. Christensen, *Edward Bulwer-Lytton*, 222–23.
5. Ibid., 223.
6. Sarah Bradford, *Disraeli* (New York: 1983), 31–32.
7. Baker, *History*, 7:184.
8. Christensen, *Edward Bulwer-Lytton*, 225.
9. Ibid., 227.
10. Ibid.
11. Ibid., 228.
12. Ibid.
13. During the winter of 1983, the English department at San Jose State University sponsored a Bulwer-Lytton prize, inviting the public to submit samples of "bad" prose in imitation of the opening lines in Bulwer's *Paul Clifford* (1830). The contest generated enough interest to be reported in the 5 May 1983 edition of the *Wall Street Journal*.
14. Escott, *Edward Bulwer*, 340.

Selected Bibliography

PRIMARY SOURCES

While there is no complete account of the locations for Bulwer manuscripts, letters, and documents, known sites are: National Library of Scotland (Blackwood Papers); Hertford County (England) Records Office; Knebworth; and Pierpont Morgan Library (manuscripts for *Alice*, *Ernest Maltravers*, *Harold*, *Zanoni*, and parts of *The Last Days of Pompeii*).

1. Novels and Stories
The editions cited below indicate the first date of publication. More recent editions may be found in Notes and References.
Falkland. London: Henry Colburn, 1827.
Pelham; or, The Adventures of a Gentleman. 3 vols. London: Henry Colburn, 1828.
The Disowned. 3 vols. London: Henry Colburn, 1828.
Devereux: A Tale. 3 vols. London: Henry Colburn, 1829.
Paul Clifford. 3 vols. London: Henry Colburn and Richard Bentley, 1830.
Eugene Aram: A Tale. 3 vols. London: Henry Colburn, 1832.
Godolphin: A Novel. 3 vols. London: Richard Bentley, 1833.
The Pilgrims of the Rhine. London: Saunders and Otley, 1834.
The Last Days of Pompeii. 3 vols. London: Richard Bentley, 1834.
The Student: A Series of Papers. 2 vols. London: Saunders and Otley, 1835.
Rienzi; or, The Last of the Roman Tribunes. 3 vols. London: Saunders and Otley, 1835.
Ernest Maltravers. 3 vols. London: Saunders and Otley, 1837.
Alice; or, The Mysteries. A Sequel to Ernest Maltravers. 3 vols. London: Saunders and Otley, 1838.
Leila; or, The Seige of Granada and *Calderon the Courtier.* London: Longman, Orme, Brown, Green, and Longmans for Charles Heath, 1838.
Night and Morning: 3 vols. London: Saunders and Otley, 1841.
Zanoni. 3 vols. London: Saunders and Otley, 1842.
Eva: A True Story of Light and Darkness; The Ill-Omened Marriage, and Other Tales and Poems. London: Saunders and Otley, 1842.
The Last of the Barons. 3 vols. London: Saunders and Otley, 1843.
The New Timon: A Romance of London. London: Henry Colburn, 1846.
Lucretia; or, The Children of Night. 3 vols. London: Saunders and Otley, 1846.

Harold, the Last of the Saxon Kings. 3 vols. London: Richard Bentley, 1848.

The Caxtons: A Family Picture. 3 vols. London: William Blackwood and Son, 1849. Serialized in *Blackwood's Magazine* from April 1848 to October 1849.

My Novel, by Pisistratus Caxton; or, Varieties in English Life. 4 vols. London: William Blackwood and Son, 1853. Serialized in *Blackwood's Magazine* from September 1850 to January 1853.

The Haunted and the Haunters. London: William Blackwood and Son, 1857. Printed in *Blackwood's Magazine,* August 1859.

What Will He Do with It?, by Pisistratus Caxton. 4 vols. London: William Blackwood and Son, 1858. Serialized in *Blackwood's Magazine* from June 1857 to January 1859.

A Strange Story. 2 vols. London: Sampson and Low, Son & Co., 1862. Serialized in *All the Year Round* from 10 August 1861 to 8 March 1862.

The Coming Race. London: William Blackwood and Son, 1871.

The Parisians. 4 vols. London: William Blackwood and Son, 1873. Serialized in *Blackwood's Magazine* from October 1872 to January 1874.

Kenelm Chillingly: His Adventures and Opinions. 3 vols. London: William Blackwood and Son, 1873.

Pausanias the Spartan; Lionel Hastings; Rupert de Lindsay; and *Glenallan* in Robert Lytton's *Life, Letters, and Literary Remains of Edward Bulwer, Lord Lytton, by His Son.* 2 vols. London: Kegan, Paul, and Tench, 1883.

2. Poetry

Ismael: An Oriental Tale, with Other Poems. London: J. Hatchard and Son, 1820.

Delmour; or, A Tale of a Sylphid, and Other Poems. London: Carpenter and Son, 1823.

Weeds and Wildflowers. Privately printed in Paris, 1826.

O'Neill; or, The Rebel. London: Henry Colburn, 1827.

The Siamese Twins: A Satirical Tale of the Times, with Other Poems. London: Henry Colburn, 1831.

Asmodeus at Large. London: Henry Colburn, 1833.

Eva: A True Story of Light and Darkness; The Ill-Omened Marriage, and Other Tales and Poems. London: Saunders and Otley, 1842.

King Arthur. London: Henry Colburn, 1848.

St. Stephens: A Poem. London: William Blackwood and Son, 1860.

Poems, Collected and Revised. London: John Murray, 1865.

The Lost Tales of Miletus. London: William Blackwood and Son, 1866.

3. Plays

The Duchess de la Valliere. A Play in Five Acts. London: Saunders and Otley, 1836.

The Lady of Lyons; or, Love and Pride. A Play in Five Acts. London: Saunders and Otley, 1838.

Richelieu; or, The Conspiracy. A Play in Five Acts. London: Saunders and Otley, 1839.

The Sea Captain; or, The Birthright. A Drama in Five Acts. London: Saunders and Otley, 1839.

Money. A Comedy in Five Acts. London: Saunders and Otley, 1840.

Not So Bad as We Seem; or, Many Sides to a Character. A Comedy in Five Acts. London: Chapman and Hall, 1851.

Dramatic Works, Collected. London: George Routledge, 1860.

The Rightful Heir. A Drama in Five Acts. London: John Murray, 1868.

Walpole; or, Every Man Has His Price. A Comedy in Rhyme, in Three Acts. London: William Blackwood and Son, 1869.

Darnley. London: George Routledge and Sons, 1882.

4. Prose Works and Translations

England and the English. 2 vols. London: Richard Bentley, 1833.

Letter to a Late Cabinet Minister on the Present Crisis. London: Richard Bentley, 1834.

Athens, Its Rise and Fall, with Views of the Literature, Philosophy, and Social Life of the Athenian People. 2 vols. London: Saunders and Otley, 1837.

The Poems and Ballads of Schiller, Translated, with a Brief Sketch of Schiller's Life. 2 vols. London: William Blackwood and Son, 1844.

Confessions of a Water-Patient, in a Letter to William Harrison Ainsworth, Editor of the "New Monthly Magazine." London: Henry Colburn, 1845.

A Word to the Public. London: Saunders and Otley, 1847.

Letters to John Bull, Esq., on Affairs Connected with His Landed Property and the Persons Who Live Thereon. London: Chapman and Hall, 1851.

Poems and Ballads of Schiller. London: William Blackwood and Son, 1852.

Caxtoniana: A Series of Essays on Life, Literature, and Manners. 2 vols. London: William Blackwood and Son, 1863.

Miscellaneous Prose Works. 3 vols. London: Richard Bentley, 1868.

The Odes and Epodes of Horace. A Metrical Translation into English, with Introduction and Commentaries. London: William Blackwood, 1869.

5. Collected Editions

Library Edition. 40 vols. Edinburgh and London: William Blackwood and Son, 1859–74.

Knebworth Edition. 37 vols. London: George Routledge and Sons, 1873–77.

New Library Edition. 40 vols. Boston: Estes and Lauriat, 1892–1893.
New Knebworth Edition. 29 vols. London: George Routledge and Sons, 1895–98. Most complete edition of Bulwer's works.

6. Letters
Devey, Louisa. *The Letters of the Late Edward Bulwer, Lord Lytton, to His Wife.* New York: G. W. Dillingham, 1889. Provides an account of Bulwer's relationship with his wife up to 1836.
Ursey, Malcolm Orthell, ed. "The Letters of Sir Edward Bulwer-Lytton to the Editors of *Blackwood's Magazine,* 1840–1873 in the National Library of Scotland." Ph.D. diss., Texas Technological College, 1963. Documents Bulwer's growing political conservatism and his pleasure in being a "Maga" writer.
Wolff, Robert Lee. "Devoted Disciple: The Letters of Mary Elizabeth Braddon to Sir Edward Bulwer-Lytton, 1862–1873." *Harvard Library Bulletin* 22 (1974):5–35; 129–61. Shows the extent of Bulwer's literary influence on M. E. B. between 1860 and 1873.

SECONDARY SOURCES

1. Bibliography
Sadleir, Michael. *XIX Century Fiction, A Bibliographical Record.* 2 vols. New York: Cooper Square, 1951. Full and accurate list of Bulwer's first editions.

2. Biographies
Escott, Thomas Hay Sweet. *Edward Bulwer, First Baron Lytton of Knebworth: A Social, Personal, and Political Monograph.* London: George Routledge and Sons, Ltd., 1910. Contains solid criticism of Bulwer's writings. Most accurate of the early biographies.
Flower, Sibylla Jane. *Bulwer-Lytton: An Illustrated Life of the First Baron Lytton, 1803–1873.* Aylesbury, England: Shire Publishing Co., 1973. Brief survey but Flower is at work on what will be the definitive modern biography.
Lytton, Robert, first earl of. *The Life, Letters, and Literary Remains of Edward Bulwer, Lord Lytton, by His Son.* 2 vols. London: Kegan Paul Tench, 1883. Reprints many of Bulwer's early pieces.
Lytton, Victor Alexander, second earl of. *The Life of Edward Bulwer, First Lord Lytton, by His Grandson.* 2 vols. London: Macmillan, 1913. Best biography to date.
———. *Bulwer-Lytton.* Denver: Allan Swallow, 1948. Good short account of Bulwer's life with excellent critical analysis of his fiction.

Sadleir, Michael. *Bulwer: A Panorama: Edward and Rosina, 1803–1836.*
Boston: Little, Brown, 1931. Only covers Bulwer's life and writings
to 1836. Had Sadleir completed the biography it would have superseded
all others. First volume provides a sound analysis of Bulwer's early
writings and relates his work to the regency and early Victorian
literary world. One of the best books on Bulwer.

3. Critical Studies

Baker, Ernest A. *The History of the English Novel.* Vol. 7. London: H. F.
and G. Witherby, 1936. Fairly complete coverage of Bulwer's novels
by a critic who grudgingly admits Bulwer's importance to early Victorian fiction.

Bell, E. G. *Introduction to the Prose Romances, Plays and Comedies of Edward
Bulwer, Lord Lytton.* Chicago: W. M. Hill, 1914. Early appraisal of
Bulwer's writings that is laudatory but brief in its analysis.

Blake, Robert. "Bulwer-Lytton." *Cornhill Magazine,* no. 1077 (1973):67–
76. Sympathetic reappraisal of Bulwer on the centenary of his death.

—————. *Disraeli.* New York: St. Martin's Press, 1967. Confined to Bulwer's part in Tory politics; fails to treat Bulwer's literary association
with Disraeli.

Bradford, Sarah. *Disraeli.* New York: Stein and Day, 1983. Provides a
good account of Bulwer's role as Disraeli's literary mentor in the early
1830s.

Buckley, Jerome Hamilton. *Season of Youth: The Bildungsroman from Dickens
to Golding.* Cambridge: Harvard University Press, 1974. Important
genre study of the bildungs formula in English fiction. Discusses
Ernest Maltravers as an early example of the bildungs pattern in the
English novel.

Cazamian, Louis. *The Social Novel in England, 1830–1850: Dickens, Disraeli, Mrs. Gaskell, Kingsley.* London: Routledge and Kegan Paul,
1973. Pioneering account of the theme of utilitarianism in the English
novel. Treats several of Bulwer's social novels.

Christensen, Allan Conrad. *Edward Bulwer-Lytton: The Fiction of New
Regions.* Athens: The University of Georgia Press, 1976. Important
modern study of Bulwer's novels brilliantly interpreted through Jung-
ian literary analysis.

Dahl, Curtis. "Benjamin Disraeli and Edward Bulwer-Lytton." In *Victorian
Fiction: A Guide to Research,* edited by Lionel Stevenson, 35–43.
Cambridge: Harvard University Press, 1966. Survey of Bulwer studies—texts, editions, biographies, bibliographies, and critical works—
published from Bulwer's death in 1873 to the early 1960s. Useful
guide for anyone wishing further sources on Bulwer.

————. "Bulwer-Lytton and the School of Catastrophe." *Philosophical Quarterly* 32 (1953):428–42. Describes how various paintings were central to Bulwer's creation of *The Last Days of Pompeii.*

————. "*Edward Bulwer-Lytton.*" In *Victorian Fiction: A Second Guide to Research*, ed. George H. Ford, 28–33. New York: The Modern Language Association of America, 1978. Covers new material since 1966.

————. "History on the Hustings: Bulwer-Lytton's Historical Novels of Politics." In *From Jane Austen to Joseph Conrad,* edited by Robert C. Rathburn and Martin Steinmann, Jr., 60–71. Minneapolis: University of Minnesota Press, 1958. Shows how Bulwer used historical analysis of the past to comment on contemporary social conditions.

————. "Recreations of Pompeii." *Archaeology* 9 (1956):182–91. Treats literary and artistic sources for Bulwer's *The Last Days of Pompeii.*

Eigner, Edwin M. "Bulwer-Lytton and the Changed Ending of *Great Expectations.*" *Nineteenth-Century Fiction* 25 (1970):104–08. Documents Bulwer's influence on the variant endings of Dickens's *Great Expectations.*

————. *The Metaphysical Novel in England and America: Dickens, Bulwer, Hawthorne, Melville.* Berkeley: University of California Press, 1978. Best account of metaphysical fiction in print. Treats Bulwer's important contribution to the genre.

————. "Raphael in Oxford Street: Bulwer's Accommodation to the Realists." In *The Nineteenth-Century Writer and His Audience,* edited by Harold Orel and George J. Worth, 61–74. Lawrence: University of Kansas Humanistic Studies, no. 40, 1969. Important account of Bulwer's theory of domestic fiction.

Fleishman, Avrom. *The English Historical Novel: Walter Scott to Virginia Woolf.* Baltimore: Johns Hopkins Press, 1971. Excellent study of historical fiction. Treats Bulwer as one of Scott's successors.

Fradin, Joseph I. " 'The Absorbing Tyranny of Every-day Life': Bulwer-Lytton's *A Strange Story.*" *Nineteenth-Century Fiction* 16 (1961):1–16. Sound analysis of Bulwer's occult novel, tracing his part in the controversy over scientific materialism.

Hollingsworth, Keith. *The Newgate Novel, 1830–1847: Bulwer, Ainsworth, Dickens, and Thackeray.* Detroit: Wayne State University Press, 1963. Solid account of Bulwer's crime novels and the *Fraser's* attack on Bulwer.

Honan, Park. Introduction to *Falkland,* edited by Herbert Van Thal, vii–xviii. London: Cassel, 1967. Useful analysis of Bulwer's early Byronic romance.

Houghton, Walter E., ed. *The Wellesley Index to Victorian Periodicals, 1824–1900.* Vol. 1. Toronto and London: University of Toronto Press,

1966. Provides dates for all Bulwer's novels serialized in *Blackwood's Magazine* and for early journalism in "Maga."

Howe, Susanne. *Wilhelm Meister and His English Kinsmen: Apprentices to Life.* New York: Columbia University Press, 1930. Early scholarly study of the bildungsroman formula.

Kaplan, Fred. *Dickens and Mesmerism: The Hidden Springs of Fiction.* Princeton: Princeton University Press, 1975. Sound account of the Victorian occult world and Dickens's interest in it. Touches only marginally on Bulwer.

Kelly, Richard. "The Haunted House of Bulwer-Lytton." *Studies in Short Fiction* 8 (1971):581–87. Useful analysis of Bulwer's classic haunted house story.

Lansbury, Coral. *Arcady in Australia: The Evocation of Australia in Nineteenth-Century English Literature.* Carlton: Melbourne University Press, 1970. Helpful in understanding Bulwer's part in fashioning the Australian myth in his fiction.

Lilijegren, S. B. *Bulwer-Lytton's Novels and Isis Unveiled.* Cambridge: Harvard University Press, 1957. Argues that Bulwer's occult novels may have been central in founding the Theosophical Society.

Lloyd, Michael. "Bulwer-Lytton and the Idealising Principle." *English Miscellany* 7 (1956):25–39. Early account of Bulwer's aesthetic of the ideal and the real.

Qualls, Barry. *The Secular Pilgrims of Victorian Fiction: The Novel as Book of Life.* Cambridge: Cambridge University Press, 1982. Treats Bulwer's part in writing double-plot metaphysical fiction.

Rosa, Matthew Whiting. *The Silver-Fork School: Novels of Fashion Preceding "Vanity Fair."* New York: Columbia University Press, 1936. Useful account of Bulwer as a silver-fork novelist during the period 1829–38.

Sanders, Andrew. *The Victorian Historical Novel, 1840–1880.* London: The Macmillan Press, 1978. Treats Bulwer's role as one of Scott's disciples in historical fiction. Focuses on Bulwer's *Harold,* but rates it an artistic failure despite Bulwer's serious historical analysis.

Simmons, James C. "Bulwer and Vesuvius: The Topicality of *The Last Days of Pompeii.*" *Nineteenth-Century Fiction* 24 (1969):103–05. Argues that part of Bulwer's success rests on Vesuvius's eruption the year Bulwer's book was published.

———. "The Novelist as Historian: An Unexplored Tract of Victorian Historiography." *Victorian Studies* 14 (1971):293–305. Useful study of Bulwer's theory of historical analysis.

Stevenson, Lionel. *The English Novel: A Panorama.* Boston: Houghton Mifflin Co., 1960. Sympathetic account of Bulwer's novels by a major historian of the English novel.

Stewart, C. Nelson. *Bulwer-Lytton as Occultist.* London: Theosophical Publishing House, 1927. Early study of Bulwer's interest in the occult. Superseded by Wolff.

Sutherland, J. A. *Victorian Novelists and Publishers.* Chicago: University of Chicago Press, 1967. Useful account of Bulwer's relationship with his publishers. Some information about the publishing history of his novels.

Wagner, Geoffrey. "A Forgotten Satire: Bulwer-Lytton's *The Coming Race.*" *Nineteenth-Century Fiction* 19 (1965):379–85. Sound analysis of Bulwer's antidemocratic thesis in *The Coming Race.*

Watts, Harold H. "Lytton's Theories of Prose Fiction." *PMLA* 50 (1935):274–89. Early study of Bulwer's theory of fiction. Superseded by Christensen and Eigner.

Wolff, Robert Lee. *Sensational Victorian: The Life and Fiction of Mary Elizabeth Braddon.* New York: Garland Publishing, 1979. Traces Bulwer's role as Miss Braddon's literary mentor.

————. *Strange Stories and Other Explorations in Victorian Fiction.* Boston: Gambit Press, 1971. Brilliant study of Bulwer's knowledge of the occult. Contains the best analysis to date of *Zanoni, Strange Story,* and *The Coming Race.* One of the most important pieces of scholarship in modern Bulwer studies.

Index

Addison, Richard, 92
Age, the, 27
Agrippa, Heinrich Cornelius, 110
Ainsworth, William Harrison, 39, 90, 111, 130, 132, 133
All the Year Round, 121
Allen, Grant, 127
Allison, Archibald, 70
Althorpe, Lord, 12
Anastasius (Hope), 27
Armadale (Collins), 52
Ashburner, Dr. John, 110
Athenaeum, the, 46, 50, 53, 117, 125
Atlas, the, 27
Auldjo, John, 36
Austen, Jane, 134

Baker, Ernest A., 101, 103, 106, 130
Barnaby Rudge (Dickens), 75
Beggar's Opera, The (Gay), 38
Bellamy, Edward, 133
Bentham, Jeremy, 55
Bentley, Richard, 57, 85
Bildungsroman, 62, 63, 68, 87, 95, 102, 131
Biran, Pierre Maine de, 121–22
Blackwood, John, 94, 100, 106
Blackwood's Magazine, 43, 65, 67, 70, 94, 100, 101, 106, 118
Blessington, Lady Marguerite, 75–76, 79, 130, 131
Boldrewood, Rolf, 133
Bolingbroke, Lord, 36–37
Bowen, Sir George, 17
Braddon, Mary Elizabeth, 52
Bradford, Sarah, 130
Brontë, Anne, 85
Brontë, Charlotte, 134
Browning, Robert, 2
Buller, Charles, 4
Bulver, Turold, 1
Bulwer-Lytton, Lord Edward George Earle

WORKS—FICTION:
Alice: or, The Mysteries, 9–10, 62–64, 69, 131

"Asmodeus at Large" (in *The Student*), 126
Calderon the Courtier, 10, 79, 80–81
Caxtons, The: A Family Picture, 15, 50, 91, 94–100, 106, 108, 129, 132, 133
Coming Race, The, 19, 65, 68, 125–27, 129, 133
"De Lindsay," 23, 24
Devereux, 9, 22, 23, 35, 36–37, 71, 131
Disowned, The, 1, 9, 23, 31–35, 37, 38, 55–56, 131
Ernest Maltravers, 9–10, 62–64, 69, 131
Eugene Aram, 9, 38, 44–47, 51, 55–56, 57, 59, 60, 131
Falkland, 5, 8, 22–23, 24–26, 131
"Glenallan," 22, 23, 24
Godolphin, 9, 57–60, 69
Greville: A Satire upon Fine Life, 23, 35–36
Harold, the Last of the Saxon Kings, 15, 85–88, 89, 90, 129, 132
"Haunted and the Haunters, The," 118–21, 124, 127, 129
"Ideal World, The" (in *Pilgrims of the Rhine*), 60–61
Kenelm Chillingly: His Adventures and Opinions, 4, 19, 21, 64, 68–69, 125, 129
Last Days of Pompeii, The, 9, 56, 71, 72–76, 77, 89, 132
Last of the Barons, The, 15, 81–85, 89, 90, 128
Leila; or, The Seige of Granada, 10, 78–80
"Linda," 23, 24
Lionel Hastings, 3, 6
Lucretia; or, The Children of the Night, 15, 38, 50–54, 94
"Monos and Diamonos" (in *The Student*), 45
"Mortimer; or, The Memoirs of a Gentleman," 23, 27
My Novel, 15, 69, 91, 100–5, 108, 129, 132
Night and Morning, 15, 38, 47–50, 131
Parisians, The, 19, 64–67, 68, 69, 125, 129
Paul Clifford, 9, 13, 38–44, 46, 55, 57, 128, 130–31
Pausanias the Spartan, 19, 88–90

152

DATE DUE

MAY 1 9 '71	MAY 17 '71		
GAYLORD			PRINTED IN U.S.A.